WONDERS OF MAN

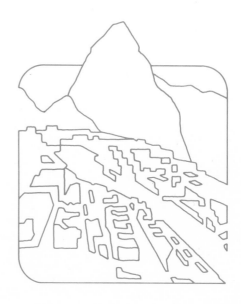

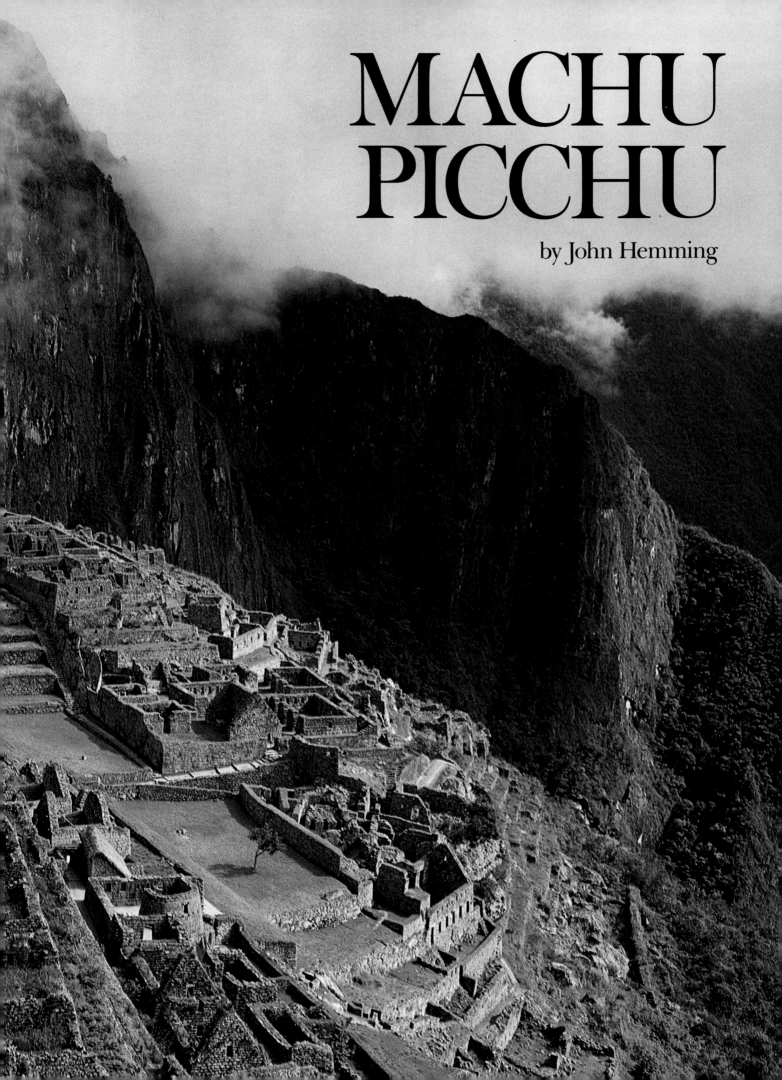

MACHU PICCHU

by John Hemming

NEWSWEEK BOOK DIVISION

Edwin D. Bayrd, Jr. *Editor*
Mary Ann Joulwan *Art Director*
Laurie P. Winfrey *Picture Editor*
Eva Galan *Copy Editor*

Alvin Garfin *Publisher*

WONDERS OF MAN
Milton Gendel *Consulting Editor*

ENDSHEETS: *Like their Peruvian ancestors, the Incas were renowned for the quantity and quality of their textiles, as multifarious in design and sophisticated in execution as any ever produced. This detail from an Indian mantle combines cut-work and embroidery.*

OPPOSITE: *Inca artistry extended to the most mundane objects, among them this* kero, *or wooden goblet, which the woodcarver's skill has transformed into an enigmatic, impassive* orejon, *or "big-eared" Inca nobleman.*

Library of Congress Cataloging in Publication Data
Hemming, John, 1935–
  Machu Picchu

  (Wonders of man)
  Bibliography: p.
  Includes index.
  1. Machu Picchu, Peru. 2. Incas.
I. Title.
F3429.1.M3H45   985'.37   80-82066
ISBN 0-88225-302-6

Printed and bound in Japan.

Contents

Introduction

It is hard to overestimate the orderliness of the Incas, a docile, obedient people led by able administrators who preferred to annex territory through shows of arms rather than force itself. And it is equally hard to overstate the rapacity and brutality of the Spanish adventurers who conquered the Inca empire in 1534 under the leadership of Francisco Pizarro, an illiterate, illegitimate brigand with an appetite for gratuitous cruelty. As one chronicler of the Conquest was to observe, "Spaniards and Indians are diametrically opposed. The Indian is by nature without greed and the Spaniard is extremely greedy, the Indian phlegmatic and the Spaniard excitable, the Indian humble and the Spaniard arrogant, the Indian deliberate in all he does and the Spaniard quick in all he wants."

By the close of the sixteenth century the greedy, excitable, arrogant Spaniards had stripped the Inca realm of its wealth and enslaved its populace. They took everything they came across, from gold to grain stores—but they did not come across everything. One entire city escaped their depredations, a mountain-top citadel that the natives called Machu Picchu. For five centuries it lay amoldering beneath a blanket of jungle growth, abandoned by the Incas and undiscovered by the conquistadores. Then, in 1911, a young American named Hiram Bingham happened upon the site—and the Lost City of the Incas, one of South America's most durable legends and one of this century's most extraordinary archaeological finds, was reclaimed by history. (Among the Indians Bingham encountered and photographed were these four women, decendants of the docile, obedient people who built Machu Picchu.) This engrossing volume is the story of that lost city, and of the men who built it.

THE EDITORS

11

MACHU PICCHU IN HISTORY

I

Lost City of the Incas

It was on July 24, 1911, that a young American named Hiram Bingham discovered the ruins of Machu Picchu. Bingham was, in a sense, a natural-born discoverer, endowed with all the right attributes for locating long-lost Inca monuments in the dense jungles of southern Peru. He was full of enthusiasm and curiosity, was brave and tough, and was both a historian and a mountaineer. He was also phenomenally lucky.

Bingham, who was born in Honolulu and educated at Yale, the University of California, and Harvard, was not only well-educated but also well-traveled by contemporary standards. Just the sort of young man, in fact, who might be expected to turn up in Peru in 1909 for a tour of Inca ceremonial sites. So enthusiastic was Bingham about what he saw on that initial expedition that he could talk of little else at a subsequent Yale class reunion; and so infectious was his enthusiasm that Bingham's fellow alumni helped him persuade the university to finance the expedition of 1911. That exploratory party, which set out from the ancient Inca capital of Cuzco (see map, page 38) in early July with a small train of horses, mules, and native porters, had a very specific goal in mind, one that had eluded other teams of archaeologists and adventurers for centuries. Bingham had seen the great Inca ruins of the Cuzco plateau; what he wanted to find was the legendary Vilcabamba, the so-called last citadel of the Incas, the final refuge of a great prince and his retinue. The mountain fastness to which Manco Inca and his court had fled in 1537 to escape the advancing conquistadores was believed to lie somewhere to the north of Cuzco, up the valley of the raging Urubamba River, deep within the all but impenetrable Andean jungle.

Despite its forbidding topography, the area north of Cuzco was well known to Peruvian natives—and no less well known to those Peruvians descended from the Spanish soldiers who had conquered the Inca empire four centuries earlier. The locals knew the trails, and they knew that none led to the long-sought citadel. However, Bingham providentially elected to follow a freshly cut trail running along the Urubamba near Cuzco.

The Peruvian government had only recently blasted a rough trail along this hitherto unpenetrated stretch of the river, and Bingham's was the first group of serious investigators to use the new route. For the first few miles the river plunged between mighty granite cliffs, then dropped into a region of jungle-clad and mist-shrouded mountains. Here the open, fertile highlands of Peru, once the homeland of the Incas, gave way to the forests of the Amazon. Bingham was struck by the soaring beauty and savage contrasts of the region he was penetrating. The brown waters of the Urubamba swirling beneath granite cliffs and snowy peaks reminded him of the Rockies; the area's tropical lushness, of his native Hawaii. "Not only has it great snow peaks looming above the clouds more than two miles overhead; gigantic precipices of many-colored granite rising sheer for thousands of feet above the foaming, glistening, roaring rapids," he later wrote; "it has also, in striking contrast, orchids and tree ferns, the delectable beauty of luxurious vege-

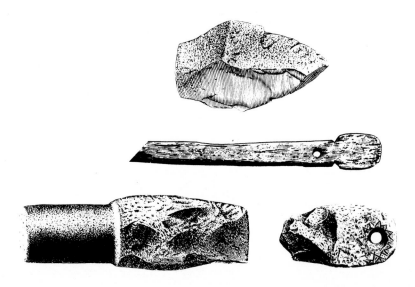

From top: scraping tool, bone awl, two stone pegs—all recovered by Bingham's party at Machu Picchu.

tation, and the mysterious witchery of the jungle."

On the night of July 23–24 the Bingham expedition camped between the new trail and the Urubamba River. A local farmer asked the purpose of their foray, and when he was told that the group was seeking Inca ruins he said that there were excellent ones in the jungle on top of the opposite mountain. Bingham decided that he must investigate this first lead and set out with the farmer and one other companion the next morning. They crept across the plunging river on a spindly bridge of logs fastened to boulders and then clambered up a rough path through the forest, pausing for lunch in a clearing 2,000 feet above the river. After eating, Bingham set off again—somewhat unenthusiastically in the intense heat and humidity—and soon came upon his first thrilling sight—a magnificent flight of stone terraces climbing for almost 1,000 feet up the mountainside. The afternoon's heat was soon forgotten as Bingham began to climb, and an hour later, in the deep jungle above these terraces, Bingham made a breathtaking discovery. There, amid the dark trees and tangled undergrowth, he saw building after building, including a three-sided temple whose granite blocks were cut with amazing beauty and precision. "I suddenly found myself in a maze of beautiful granite houses!" Bingham would later write of this ecstatic moment. And, as he investigated each successive archaeological treasure in this lost city set on its steep, forested ridge, he observed, "They were covered with trees and mosses and the growth of centuries, but in the dense shadow, hiding in bamboo thickets and tangled vines, could be seen, here and there, walls of white granite ashlars most carefully cut and exquisitely fitted together." Bingham's expedition was only a few days old and already it had, unearthed what are certainly the most famous ruins in all of South America, Machu Picchu.

The search for the last refuge of the Incas, Vilcabamba, dates at least from the time of the Peruvian chronicler Cosme Bueno, who wrote in 1768 that "a few years ago some people, attracted by a tradition that there was an ancient town called Choquequirau, crossed the Apurimac on rafts and penetrated the mountain forests. They found a deserted place built of quarried stone, covered in woods and very hot. Sumptuous houses and palaces were recognized." And in the early nineteenth century, shortly after Peru gained its independence from Spain, a local landowner called Tejada reportedly searched for buried treasure, presumably objects made of gold and silver, in the Inca ruin.

Choquequirau received its first serious visitor, the Comte de Sartiges, in 1834. The eminent French explorer approached Choquequirau by a tortuous and difficult route. He began by crossing a high mountain pass between the snow-clad peaks of Soray and Salcantay (see map inset, page 38), then cut his way along abandoned trails to a hacienda on the Urubamba well downstream of Machu Picchu—passing within miles of its magnificent ruins, without suspecting their existence—before he *re-crossed* the Vilcabamba hills, cutting his way through unpenetrated jungles in order to descend, finally,

Following a final, foredoomed attempt to drive the invading conquistadores from their homeland—a gallant rising crushed by Spanish troops in 1537— the last remnants of the Inca army retreated into the virtually impenetrable Amazonian rain-forest northwest of Cuzco, their fallen capital. Led by Manco Inca himself, the exiles made their way along the roiling watercourse of the Urubamba River (opposite), ultimately settling at a place called Vilcabamba. Nearly four centuries later a young American archaeologist named Hiram Bingham was to set out along this same route, determined to rediscover the long-lost city of Vilcabamba, the legendary last citadel of the Incas.

to the ruins of Choquequirau, perched above the Apurimac. The hapless explorer and his party suffered from exhaustion and thirst as they cut through tangles of high grass and spiny bamboos. The flies and mosquitoes were so terrible that the men had to sleep in the midst of a ring of smoking brushwood with their heads completely buried under thick blankets. Before returning to Cuzco the expedition spent a week clearing some of the undergrowth from this Inca ruin, and the Comte de Sartiges left convinced that Choquequirau was the last refuge of the Incas.

Another French explorer—history records only his surname, Angrand—managed to reach this same nearly inaccessible ruin after 1850, lured to it by a rumor that, in his words, "immense treasures were buried among the ruins when the last survivors of the race of the sun retired to this savage asylum." Angrand measured and sketched the Inca buildings at Choquequirau, and in so doing he noticed a terrace wall of Inca niches. He decided that treasure might be behind this Egyptian-looking screen, and ordered his men to tear an ugly hole in the Inca masonry—revealing nothing but earth behind. The explorer also noticed a row of stone rings embedded in another stone wall, and he concluded that these must have been used to tether pumas or jaguars—the only wild Peruvian animals that would have needed such powerful restraints.

During the last half of the nineteenth century Choquequirau became firmly established in the popular imagination as the lost city of Vilcabamba, and various travelers tried in vain to reach the elusive ruin whose exact location had been lost in the intervening decades since the visits of the Comte de Sartiges and Angrand. Then, in the early years of this century, a Peruvian official named J. J. Nuñez mounted an enormous expedition to relocate Choquequirau–"Vilcabamba." This government-sponsored sortie approached the putative site of the lost city from the south side of the mighty Apurimac canyon. A brave old Chinese in the party managed to swim across the swirling waters and secure a line to the far bank so that a suspension bridge could be built. Nuñez's expedition spent the next three months cutting a zigzag path up 6,000 feet of slippery and densely forested mountainside on the far bank—and succeeded in reaching the ruins. Having reclaimed Choquequirau for all time from the enveloping mists of ancient history and the smothering embrace of tropical liana, Nuñez's men cleared and thoroughly investigated the Inca city, making no dramatic discoveries in the process. It was becoming increasingly clear, however, that these remains were not Vilcabamba. Shortly afterward, in 1909, the young Hiram Bingham was able to cross Nuñez's bridge to visit Choquequirau. It was Bingham's first glimpse of Inca ruins—and the sight fired his enthusiasm.

Now, two years later, as Bingham and his men surveyed their ridge-top discovery, they naturally speculated on whether *they* had found the famous lost city of the Incas. It was a well-known historical fact that when the Inca empire was overthrown by the Spanish in 1533 one Inca prince, Manco, fled with some of his subjects to a retreat in the wild

hills north of Cuzco. For thirty-five years Manco Inca and his sons ruled this tiny kingdom of Vilcabamba—a reminder, at once proud and pitiful, of their lost empire. A number of Spanish envoys and missionaries visited the city during its brief period of independent native rule; their visits ceased when a powerful Spanish military expedition conquered Vilcabamba in 1572. The last of Manco's sons was captured and taken to Spanish-occupied Cuzco for execution, and his abandoned jungle capital was soon forgotten, overgrown by vegetation.

The Peruvian historians whom Hiram Bingham consulted before setting out in search of the lost citadel of the Incas told him that extant sixteenth-century chronicles identified a number of place names in connection with Manco Inca's short-lived kingdom of Vilcabamba. There was, for example, a town and palace called Vitcos that had been Manco's first capital after he fled Cuzco. But when a Spanish raiding party penetrated as far as Vitcos in 1537, Manco determined that the site was too exposed—and therefore ordered the construction of a new capital, called Vilcabamba. This second site was more remote and more easily defended—and yet a mere two days' march from Vitcos (at a time when the trails were clear and the bridges intact). The Peruvian scholars convinced Bingham that Choquequirau did not fit surviving sixteenth-century descriptions of either city; the citadel that the Comte de Sartiges had found was not, in fact, the Vilcabamba that Manco Inca had founded. In Lima, the historian Carlos Romero urged Bingham to seek other ruins—and actually suggested where

he might look. In his first attempt to comply with Romero's advice by investigating local reports of "other ruins," Bingham was to happen upon the incomparable wonders of Machu Picchu.

Bingham's problem now was to identify the ruins he had found. He and his men surveyed the site and returned for two successive seasons to clear the jungle growth from Machu Picchu's tumbled masonry. This was arduous work, for in places, as Bingham reported, "massive trees, two feet thick, perched on the gable ends of small, beautifully constructed houses." Although the American explorer paid his men relatively well, there were continual desertions by local Indians reluctant to labor on the rain-drenched hillside in the humid forest. Workers were also lost to snakebite, for the tangled undergrowth concealed deadly coral snakes and "lance-head" bushmasters. While cataloging descriptions of each of Machu Picchu's temples, palaces, and houses, Bingham persuaded his men to comb the hillside for burial caves—a search that yielded some fifty burial sites. By the end of his excavations and explorations, Bingham had scoured "every accessible—and many seemingly inaccessible—parts of Huayna Picchu and Machu Picchu mountains and the ridge between them." From all this Bingham concluded that he had in fact discovered the lost city of Vilcabamba. He declared, at first hesitatingly and later with growing conviction, that this wonderful ruin, now known as Machu Picchu, had once been Manco Inca's citadel. The general public accepted Bingham's assertion unhesitatingly; scholars, with varying degrees of reluc-

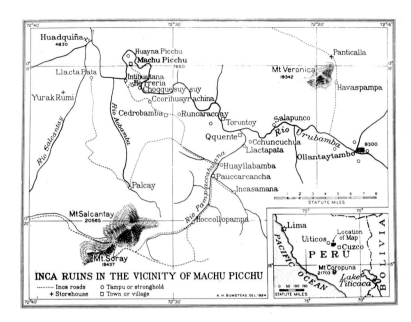

INCA RUINS IN THE VICINITY OF MACHU PICCHU
------- Inca roads o Tampu or stronghold
+ Storehouse □ Town or village
A. H. BUMSTEAD DEL. 1924.

tance. And, always, the question remained: Had Bingham in fact succeeded in locating the lost city of the Incas, or was Vilcabamba still to be found? The answer was to be divined from contemporary documents, further explorations, and a careful study of Machu Picchu itself.

One chronicler—as Spaniards who recorded the events of the Conquest and of Inca history were called—stated that the jungle hills and mountains around Machu Picchu had been conquered in the mid-fifteenth century by the Inca ruler Pachacuti. This was a man of undisputed genius who is generally credited with having devised the Incas' system of government *and* religion, and it was he who propelled a mountain tribe into its dazzling burst of imperial expansion. Pachacuti was the Alexander, the Napoleon of the Incas, a successful conqueror who had the energy to supervise every detail of the administration of his empire. (Indeed, Pachacuti's name may have meant "Reformer of the World" in the Inca tongue.) As the Jesuit chronicler Bernabé Cobo wrote, Pachacuti "instituted the state with a code of laws and statutes.... He set everything in order: he abolished some rites and ceremonies and added others. He expanded the official religion, instituting sacrifices and services by which the gods were to be worshipped. He embellished the temples with magnificent buildings.... In short, he overlooked nothing and organised everything efficiently."

Before Pachacuti, the Incas were only one of scores of tribes that occupied particular valleys or regions in the long chain of the Andes mountains.

Inca legends described a migration by this tribe from the high plateau of Lake Titicaca, which lies on the border between modern Peru and Bolivia, northward to the rich mountain valleys around Cuzco. The legendary brothers who organized this migration established a dynasty of tribal rulers known by the same name as their tribe: Inca. Pachacuti was the eighth ruler in this line, which would mean that the Incas occupied Cuzco no earlier than the thirteenth century of the Christian era—a fact confirmed by archaeological dating of Inca and pre-Inca objects excavated in the region. Once established at Cuzco, however, the Inca tribe prospered and expanded into the surrounding districts through a combination of successful skirmishes and marriages with the families of other chieftains.

According to the chronicler Miguel Cabello Balboa, the event that was to transform Inca history occurred in A.D. 1438, when the powerful Chanca tribe invaded Inca lands from the west, apparently intent upon capturing the town of Cuzco. With the enemy at their walls, the Inca ruler Viracocha fled with his eldest son. It was left to a younger son—Pachacuti—to rally the Inca forces and lead them to an unexpected victory over the Chanca. This success seemed so clearly miraculous that the Incas attributed it to divine intervention, saying that stones on the battlefield had risen up and been transformed into warriors who fought with the victorious Incas. Pachacuti was chosen as the new Inca ruler, and he soon embarked on a headlong career of conquest and social reorganization. His first campaign, as already noted, was north into the wild

The Incas were marvelously skilled masons, and the masterfully cut and joined walls and roadbeds they constructed

e still in service today, their beauty and strength undiminished by five centuries of constant use.

hills beyond Machu Picchu—possibly a strategic move to prevent the defeated Chanca from occupying that remote region. Before long, the Inca armies were to invade the homelands of the Chanca themselves—and then those of the Colla and Lupaca peoples, near Lake Titicaca. The Incas were poised to strike northward and southward for hundreds of miles along the line of the Andes and the western coast of South America. Under Pachacuti's guidance they had entered a phase of seemingly uncheckable expansion. And, as the secretary to the Spanish conquerer of Peru, Francisco Pizarro, would confirm in 1532, this Inca military expansion had occurred relatively recently: "by the reckoning of the most ancient men, this land had been subject to an [Inca] prince for only ninety years."

The first part of Machu Picchu that Hiram Bingham saw in 1911 was a great flight of agricultural terraces. Such terracing was one of the great engineering triumphs of the Incas. Men had been taming the vertiginous and unstable slopes of the Andes for many centuries by terracing, but the technique was perfected by the efficient Incas. The method of construction was simple enough—a retaining wall of roughly shaped rocks was built and the space behind filled with loose rubble topped by soil—but the collective effort needed to contour entire mountainsides in this manner was prodigious. Inca terraces were admirably level, were curved to follow the hillside against which they rested, and were provided with ingenious irrigation channels and networks of connecting staircases.

Machu Picchu, as Bingham discovered, was par-

Tribes living along Peru's Pacific coast, west of the Inca homeland, subsisted on a diet rich in fish, mollusks, and crustaceans. The Incas' mountainous realm offered no such bounty, and it was only by dint of the most intensive sort of cultivation that they were able to feed themselves. Their staples were the potato (far right) and maize—which was planted in terraced beds (lower left), irrigated (middle left), and carefully tended against predators (top left) before it was harvested (near right).

ticularly well provided with agricultural terraces. So were a number of other Inca enclaves situated on the slopes above the Urubamba River between Machu Picchu and Cuzco. The ratio of agricultural terraces to farm dwellings was very high in this entire region, and it is possible that the terraces of the Urubamba valley were intended to produce an agricultural surplus to supply the Inca court in Cuzco. Or they may have been plantations, used for raising the coca bush, whose leaf yielded a mild narcotic much prized by Inca nobility.

Any great civilization depends on a regular supply of food and, more particularly, of protein. At the time of the Conquest the flora and fauna of South America were entirely different from those of Africa and Eurasia, and consequently the peoples of the protein-poor Andes were significantly less well endowed by nature than their European contemporaries. They possessed no cattle, domestic pigs, poultry, or sheep, and most of their meat came from small, rodent-like guinea pigs, which thrived in the high altitudes of the Andes and were easily fed from household scraps. Millions of these guinea pigs—whose name in Quechua, the Inca language, is *cuy,* an onomatopeic rendering of their squeak—were consumed by the Incas and other Andean peoples. Llamas and such closely related quadrupeds as alpacas, vicuñas, and guanacos—all members of the camel family—were the only other domestic animals kept in quantity by the Incas, but they were raised more for wool than meat. Llamas were also used as beasts of burden, although they were too weak to carry men or pull vehicles. Apart from these

few domestic creatures, the Incas' only other sources of meat protein were the rabbits, deer and pigeons they hunted. But such hunting was not easy for a people with no horses—or firearms—both of which were unknown in the Americas before the European invasions.

The peoples of South America were also poor in plant foods, for they had no native wheat or other cereals, no olives, rice, or grapes, and few green vegetables. Their compensation was two plants that provided the food base for the great civilizations of Mexico, Central America, and the Andes. One was maize, which had evolved during centuries of cultivation. The other was a vegetable that the chronicler Pedro de Cieza de León described as "like a truffle, and when cooked as soft inside as boiled chestnuts. Like the truffle, it has neither rind nor stone, for it also grows beneath the ground." He referred, of course, to the potato, a plant native to Peru and one that thrives there in hundreds of strains, colors, and varieties. The conquistadores, avid for Inca gold, never suspected that this humble vegetable would prove to be the greatest of the treasures of Peru—for the world's annual potato harvest far exceeds in value all the gold and silver treasures of the Inca empire.

It was with these staple foods that the peoples of the Andes multiplied in numbers and evolved their advanced civilizations. The Incas, as we have noted, were late arrivals, an obscure mountain tribe that rapidly assimilated the skills of older, more sophisticated Peruvian cultures. Although highly efficient, they were less artistic than many of the plea-

sure-loving peoples they were to conquer.

There was one field of art in which the Incas did shine: architecture, or, more particularly, stone-working. Inca masons employed some of the largest stones ever incorporated into buildings. Their structures were simple in plan and decoration but, as the chronicler Cobo wrote, "the remarkable part of [Inca] buildings was the walls—but these were so amazing that it would be difficult for any who have not seen them to appreciate them." The huge stones were cut, ground, and polished until they joined one another with the tightest possible precision: buildings, including many that have survived successive earthquakes, contain stones which interlock so perfectly that a knife cannot be forced between them. As if to proclaim this skill, the Incas countersunk the joins in their masonry, a form of rustication in which each stone bulges slightly and the joints are in shadow. The resulting pattern of light and shade provides fascinating visual relief—often amounting to decoration—to walls that would otherwise be quite bare.

The Incas had two main methods of laying their stone blocks. They arranged them either in regular courses of rectangular ashlars or in a complicated jigsaw of irregularly shaped blocks—a system known as polygonal masonry. Since most styles of building evolve from more primitive antecedents, it is supposed that the coursed method was in imitation of earlier walls made of clay bricks or adobes. The irregular polygonal style clearly derived from walls made from fieldstones, roughly chipped to fit together and held by clay mortar. And the bevel of

Inca rustication could have copied the slight bulge that occurs in drying adobes or in walls made of layers of peat. The Incas predominantly built terraces and retaining walls in the polygonal style, both for greater strength and because simple terrace walls were made of loosely fitting stones. The more precise coursed method was employed for free-standing walls.

One chronicler, writing nearly four hundred years ago, expressed the awe still experienced by anyone contemplating Inca stonework for the first time and wondering at the effort involved in making the gigantic, irregularly shaped blocks fit together with such uncanny precision:

> Even though these blocks are so extraordinarily large, they are cut with amazing skill. They are elegant and so finely positioned against one another, without mortar, that the joints are scarcely visible. I can assure you that the rusticated, polygonal walls—which may appear rougher than walls of [coursed] ashlars—seem to me to have been far more difficult to make. For, not being cut straight (apart from the outer face, which was as smooth as on the ashlars), and yet being so tightly joined to one another, one can well appreciate the amount of work involved in having them interlock in the way we see. . . . Thus, if the top of one stone makes a curve or point, there is a corresponding groove or cavity in the stone above to fit exactly into the other. Some stones have many angles and indentations all round their sides; but the stones they meet are cut in such a way that they interlock per-

The residential sections of Machu Picchu were divided into so-called clan groups, each with its private entrance—generally a simple affair such as the aperture seen at right, which is found along the city's eastern wall. The main gate of Machu Picchu was more elaborate, capped by a massive stone lintel surmounted by a ring-stone (visible at top center in the photograph at lower left). A hardwood beam, suspended from this ring-stone, is thought to have served as the principal support of the city's only formal entryway.

fectly. Such a work must have been immensely laborious! To interlock the stones against one another, it must have been necessary to remove and replace them repeatedly to test them. Since they were of such great size, it is obvious how many workers and how much suffering must have been involved!

The chronicler was absolutely right to stress the amount of patient human effort that went into the construction of such walls, for there was no secret formula, no magic chemical that could shape stones. The work was done with stone axes, the abrasion involved only sand and water, and the results spoke for the dedicated skill of the masons. The only "secret" lay in the Incas' ability to mobilize the levies needed to perform such labor, and here Bernabé Cobo, who watched the natives at work soon after the Spanish Conquest, observed that "the Indians had no iron tools or wheeled vehicles. . . . This really does cause one to be justifiably amazed. It gives some idea of the vast number of people needed [to build] these structures. We see stones of such prodigious size that a hundred men working for a month would have been inadequate to cut one of them. . . . For a lack of tools or clever devices necessarily increases the volume of labor, and the Indians had to do it all by brute force." Cobo further noted that native builders cut with obsidian and other hard stone knives, and tended to pound rather than cut in their quarrying. They moved stones by the age-old method of heaving with rope cables—along rollers if necessary. Having no pul-

leys, Inca masons raised blocks by pulling them into place up huge earthen ramps.

Another hallmark of Inca building was the trapezoidal shape of doors and window openings. The lintel, which supported the mass of wall above, was shorter than the sill, so that the side walls, or jambs, sloped inward toward the top. This produced an attractive, functional shape, one the Incas used in all their openings. Inca builders also liked niches: either full-length niches, like the sentry boxes found in the outer walls of palaces or temples, or alcove niches, set at chest height inside buildings and used for storage. Rows of niches were always spaced at regular intervals—typical of the efficient Incas—and they served to embellish otherwise plain structures.

The Incas reserved their brilliantly cut stonework for important buildings, those associated with the ruling family, imperial government, or official religion. Humble people built their houses of *tapia* (compacted mud, a form of adobe), *pirca* (roughly shaped fieldstones set in clay), or, in the hot and humid jungles, of upright wooden slats. Significantly, Machu Picchu has far more fine stonework than one would expect to find in an Inca city of its size. It was, admittedly, built on a mountain of granite, a place where stone was plentiful and the clay and straw needed for adobes were in short supply; but much of the stonework is of the finest interlocking quality, a sure sign that this was a place of particular religious or royal significance. And this, among other factors, led Hiram Bingham to the conclusion that Machu Picchu was a sanctuary of great antiquity, antedating the Incas by eight or ten centuries. In Bingham's theory, Machu Picchu had played an important role in the origin of the Inca tribe—and was therefore embellished with sacred temples by its rulers. Unhappily, at least insofar as Bingham's theory is concerned, nothing in his own excavations or in the ruined buildings of Machu Picchu supports a claim for such antiquity, for the city's structures are all of late Inca style. Undaunted, Bingham also claimed that Manco Inca and the royal fugitives who, briefly, escaped the conquistadores merely embellished the ancient holy city. "It is quite possible," he wrote, "that . . . this ancient sanctuary had to be enlarged to receive the priests and other attendants of the last Inca and the chosen women who sought refuge here in the days of Pizarro." Indeed, Bingham became so convinced of his theory that, by the 1950s, the decade of his death, he was boldly stating that "no one now disputes that this was the site of ancient Vilcabamba." But the search for Vilcabamba was not over: subsequent research and exploration were to reveal new and more convincing candidates for the site of the elusive lost city.

OVERLEAF: The men who built Machu Picchu are long gone, their place taken by visitors from all corners of the globe. But the alpacas remain, their presence a reminder of the days when the Vilcabamba cordillera belonged to the Incas, who used the alpaca's fleece to weave fabrics of unparalleled richness and its flesh to supplement a protein-poor diet of grains and root vegetables.

II

Hitching-post of the Sun

Like all who followed him up the steep slopes of the Urubamba River valley, Bingham was most impressed not by Machu Picchu's magnificent stonework, nor by its aggregation of sacred buildings, but by its outstanding natural defenses. So spectacular are those defenses that the visitor cannot help but feel that nature itself collaborated with the Incas to keep native enemies and, later, Spanish conquerors at bay. The city is built on a granite arete, a knife-sharp spine of rock running roughly north-south (see diagram, page 164). To the east and west, densely forested hillsides fall precipitously for thousands of feet before meeting the roiling waters of the Urubamba. To the north is the granite pinnacle of Huayna Picchu (Huayna means "young" or "new"; Picchu is a place name), rising like the horn of a rhinoceros at the end of the mountain spur. The only vulnerable flank is therefore to the south, and on this side the principal buildings of the inner city are protected by a dry moat and by a stone barrier comprised of terraces and windowless house walls. The main gate of Machu Picchu is located at the upper end of this man-made barrier. It has a massive stone surround with jambs that slope inward in the characteristic trapezoidal shape favored by Inca masons. On the inner walls of this gate are found what remain of its defensive features: a stone ring, set in the lintel, from which a heavy door was once suspended; and stone pegs, sunk into the side walls, that once served to support a heavy protective bar.

In Manco Inca's time Machu Picchu could be approached by only two roads—or, rather, two trails, for the Incas had no wheeled vehicles and therefore built what were, in essence, paved footpaths, used by government couriers, local peasants, and columns of domesticated llamas alike. Both approaches to Machu Picchu were well defended. One, which climbs from the floor of the Urubamba valley to a point west of Machu Picchu, was defended by a drawbridge. This narrow trail runs along the face of a sheer rock cliff, where it encounters a deliberately created gap that was evidently once spanned by a removable log bridge. The other road, which begins in Cuzco and passes a number of other ruined Inca cities, runs through the steep, forested hills above the Urubamba. This trail, now cleared and its Inca paving restored, is famous among backpackers as the Inca Trail, route of a spectacularly beautiful four-day walk to the lost city. It too was defended in ancient times—by a tunnel and by a gate above Machu Picchu. The city was further protected by a lookout, atop Huayna Picchu, that could receive warning signals from the surrounding hills.

Hiram Bingham was impressed by all these defenses, which led him—and others—to conclude that Machu Picchu was in fact a citadel, an advance outpost protecting the Inca empire from the fierce tribes of the Amazon jungle. But Paul Fejos, the American archaeologist who led a 1941 expedition to discover and excavate the ruins near Machu Picchu, came to doubt Bingham's hypothesis. In Fejos' judgment the so-called defenses of Machu Picchu, like those of neighboring sites, were militarily insignificant. He argued that, had the Incas wanted to build serious military defenses, they could cer-

Bronze knives found at Machu Picchu, including the finest example of casting discovered at site, left.

tainly have done so. Machu Picchu's dry moat and low wall, he insisted, were more symbolic than practical. Fejos interpreted them as a screen to isolate the holy city, a barrier to the unauthorized or uninitiated—and as further confirmation that Machu Picchu was a sacred place.

There were three main elements to the religion of the late Inca empire. One was the natural superstitions of a simple agricultural people. Since time immemorial, the farming tribes of the Andes had worshiped the natural features of their surroundings, attaching spiritual importance to particular springs, caves, rocky outcroppings, and the crests of mountain passes. Every village was surrounded by a cluster of these natural shrines— places that, over the centuries, had acquired magical importance. Many of these superstitions antedated the Incas, and many survive to this day. Modern Indians, for instance, still leave a symbolic offering—often something as small as an eyelash or a pebble—when they reach the top of a pass or cross a dangerous river. These simple faiths extended to any natural object that was unusual in its conformation. The Incas would venerate a curious rock, a misshapen plant or freak animal, or, in the words of one chronicler, "anything that differed from others of its kind, through some extraordinary or exaggerated feature. . . . They reasoned that if nature had marked them out there must be something miraculous involved." Like most primitive agrarian cultures the world over, the Incas also celebrated the changing seasons of the year and the important events in the agricultural calendar—the time for

sowing, the start of the spring rains, the harvest— and special ceremonies evolved for each month of the year.

A second, more sophisticated element of Inca religion was the worship of heavenly bodies. The Incas were skilled astronomers who observed and recorded the passage of the sun and other celestial spheres. Inti, the sun, was worshiped with elaborate temples and a full-time priesthood; the moon, thunder, lightning, rainbows, and the major stars were venerated with almost equal devotion. In every part of the Inca empire terraced farmlands and herds of llamas were reserved for "the sun," that is, for support of the sun god's temples and priesthood. This was a manifestation of the secular power of the state religion easily comprehended by the Spanish conquerors, for it corresponded to the extensive landholdings of the Church in Europe.

The third base of Inca religion was veneration of the royal family and their ancestors. This was a mainstay of Inca power, and one carefully fostered by the state. As with the rulers of ancient Egypt or Japan, the Inca was held to have divine status, and he was identified with the most potent celestial body, the sun. In the words of one Spanish chronicler, "the first Inca, Manco Capac . . . made up the fable that he and his wife were children of the Sun and that their father had [created] them so that they should go about the land teaching the people." To further this illusion, the first Inca wore a suit of shining metal designed to reflect the sun's rays and dazzle his followers.

Over the generations a number of places in the

empire came to be thought of as oracles—shrines where the Inca or his priests could consult the sun god or some powerful local deity. Apparently this too was the result of conscious contrivance on the part of the royal family, as the last of Manco Inca's sons to rule in Vilcabamba, Tupac Amaru, revealed in an extraordinary confession made just as he was about to be executed in Cuzco in 1572. In a speech to the crowd that had gathered around his scaffold, Tupac Amaru announced his conversion to Christianity and declared:

> All that I and my ancestors the Incas have told you up to now—that you should worship the sun and the shrines, idols, stones, rivers, mountains and caves—is completely false. When we told you that we were entering in to speak to the sun, that it advised you to do what we told you, and that it spoke, this was false. It did not speak, we alone did. For it is an object and cannot speak. My brother the Inca Titu Cusi told me that whenever I wished to tell you Indians to do something, I should enter alone to the sun idol. . . . Afterwards I should emerge and tell the Indians that it had spoken to me, and that it said whatever I wished to tell them.

With no notion of how genuine Tupac Amaru's conversion was, we cannot judge the sincerity of his final remarks, which suggest calculation of the most cynical sort on the part of the Inca and his forebears. What factors influenced the hapless ruler during his captivity we can only guess, but we do know that his remarkable denunciation of the state religion struck the Spaniards as almost too good to be true, prompting the Viceroy himself to declare: "Tupac Amaru made a confession on the scaffold which, from what is understood, was the most advantageous thing that could have occurred for the conversion of these peoples."

These three components of Inca religion were closely interwoven. Many natural shrines, for instance, were also associated with the royal family or with events in Inca history. Further, it was the Inca ruler who presided over important festivals of the agricultural calendar—and the Inca and his ancestors who were closely identified with the official worship of the sun. This connection was strengthened by the legend of Viracocha, the creator god of Inca mythology. Viracocha was said to have emerged from Lake Titicaca, south of Cuzco, and to have created the world and all living creatures. (Christian missionaries would later welcome this myth, so similar was it to their own Book of Genesis.) One of the ruling Incas, the father of the great Pachacuti, was actually called Viracocha, and there were temples to Viracocha in Cuzco and other Inca cities—a means of linking the ruling dynasty to the creator god as well as to the sun god. By evoking an aura of divinity the Incas sought to inspire blind devotion among their followers.

Awe of the Inca's majesty, coupled with a sense of patriotic duty, help to explain the triumphs of Inca building. The masons who toiled with such devotion and skill were proud to serve their divine ruler; they wanted their kings and religious leaders to enjoy the finest possible workmanship, and they

Lake Titicaca (below), which lies athwart Peru's common border with modern Bolivia, 200-odd miles southeast of Cuzco, is the highest major body of water in the world. Titicaca's distinction is more than geological, however: the ancient Incas revered the mountain-girt lake as the birthplace of Viracocha (left), the founder-god of their pantheon and the divine progenitor of the royal household. "While all was in utter darkness," Inca legend has it, there rose over Titicaca "a resplendent sun." From that sun was born Viracocha— and, with him, the Inca tradition of sun-worship. Descendants of the Incas still worship on Lake Titicaca's Island of the Sun, making the pilgrimage as their forebears did, in graceful double-prowed balsas constructed of reeds.

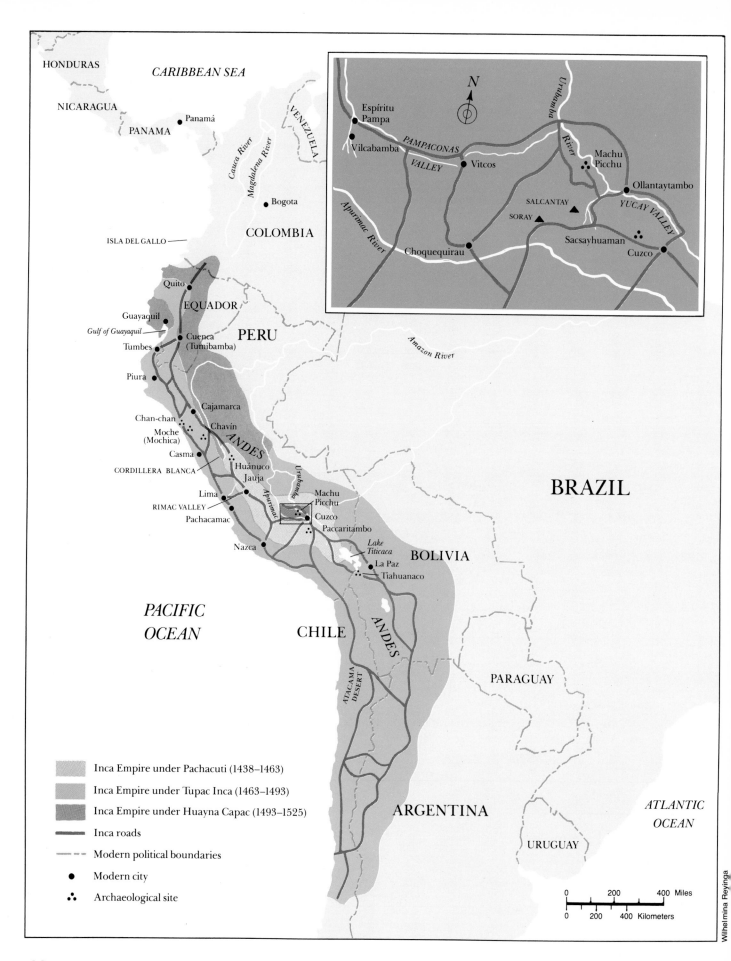

HONDURAS

CARIBBEAN SEA

NICARAGUA

PANAMA • Panamá

Cauca River

Magdalena River

VENEZUELA

• Bogota

COLOMBIA

ISLA DEL GALLO

• Quito

EQUADOR

Guayaquil •

Gulf of Guayaquil

PERU

• Cuenca (Tumibamba)

Tumbes •

Piura •

Amazon River

Cajamarca •

Chan-chan •

Moche (Mochica)

Chavín

ANDES

Casma •

CORDILLERA BLANCA

Huánuco •

Jauja •

Urubamba

Lima •

RIMAC VALLEY

Apurimac

Machu Picchu

Cuzco •

Paccaritambo •

Pachacamac •

Nazca •

Lake Titicaca

La Paz •

Tiahuanaco

BOLIVIA

BRAZIL

PACIFIC OCEAN

CHILE

ANDES

ATACAMA DESERT

PARAGUAY

ARGENTINA

URUGUAY

ATLANTIC OCEAN

Inset map (upper right):

N

Espíritu Pampa •

Vilcabamba •

PAMPACONAS VALLEY

• Vitcos

Apurimac River

Urubamba River

Machu Picchu

Ollantaytambo •

YUCAY VALLEY

SALCANTAY ▲

SORAY ▲

Choquequirau •

Sacsayhuaman

Cuzco •

Legend:

Inca Empire under Pachacuti (1438–1463)

Inca Empire under Tupac Inca (1463–1493)

Inca Empire under Huayna Capac (1493–1525)

——— Inca roads

- - - - Modern political boundaries

• Modern city

⋰ Archaeological site

0   200   400 Miles

0   200   400 Kilometers

Wilhelmina Reyinga

The rise and fall of the Inca empire confounds almost every historical verity. It was a highly advanced civilization, yet it lacked the wheel and a written language. It was the foremost military power in South America, its suzerainty stretching some 2,500 miles from what is now southern Colombia to Chile's Maule River (map opposite), yet it was conquered by a handful of Spanish adventurers. And perhaps most ironic of all, it was an agrarian society occupying some of the least arable land on the continent, ranging from rainless coastal deserts to icy, windswept mountain passes.

therefore lavished the same care on buildings associated with royalty as their contemporaries did on the cathedrals of medieval Europe. An aged Peruvian chief who was interrogated by the Spaniards at the time of the Conquest recalled how his tribe had, over the years, provided labor levies and personal servants to the Inca: "They gave [the Inca] many Indians for warfare, and to build his houses and agricultural terraces in Cuzco; male and female Indians to serve in his palace, and daughters of chiefs as his handmaidens; they gave him Indian men and women to kill in sacrifice to the idols and shrines, and Indians to settle as colonists in [conquered] places." The chief then listed the produce that his tribe had supplied, in great volume to the Inca as tribute: dehydrated potatoes and other food, fresh fish carried by runners, quantities of cloth, llamas, gold and silver from mines in their area, wool, sandals for the army, slings, copper battle axes, copper clamps for buildings, "and everything else that the Inca requested of them, *for they were very obedient to him.*"

At Machu Picchu the visitor is constantly reminded of these different strands of Inca religion. There can be little doubt that the Incas were a highly spiritual people and that Machu Picchu was a sacred place. A traveler approaching by either of the two old Inca trails entered the city from above. Most modern visitors now arrive from the Tourist Hotel that lies below the city, having driven up from the Urubamba on a zigzag road built during restoration work in 1934. For such individuals it is worth climbing the flights of stairs at the end of the first group of agricultural terraces to look down on the city from an isolated Inca building known as the Watchman's Hut. The original Inca roads joined at a point near this structure and went on to Machu Picchu's main gate. The view from here is superb, with the lost city spread out below; the sugarloaf pinnacle of Huayna Picchu beyond; the Urubamba roaring past in a tight hairpin bend, thousands of feet below; and the mysterious, jungle-clad Vilcabamba hills disappearing into the middle distance, half shrouded in tropical mists.

Beside the Watchman's Hut is an open space containing one of Machu Picchu's many sculpted outcrops, doubtless a shrine in its own right at one time. Its top has been flattened to form an altar and it has both molded protuberances and tiny access steps cut into its sides. It may have been used for the laying out of mummified bodies prior to burial—Bingham's men did find a cemetery in a nearby cave—but it was more likely used for sacrifice, since most Inca festivals included the ritual slaughter of llamas or alpacas. Elaborate rules governed the number of animals to be sacrificed at each such ceremony and even dictated their color: pure white llamas were offered up to the sun, brown ones to Viracocha, and mottled ones to thunder. (In Cuzco, a reddish animal was sacrificed daily to the sun.) The Jesuit Bernabé Cobo wrote that the Incas "prided themselves on being religious and were particularly careful about their sacrifices, so that everything they had, grew or harvested, and everything they attempted was done primarily to be dedicated and offered to their gods and shrines."

Their method of killing any animal, particularly llamas, was, in Cobo's words, "to give them a few turns around the idol, then have the priest take them with his right arm, turn their eyes toward the god to which the sacrifices were being directed, offer the appropriate prayers for the purpose, and then to decapitate the victim."

Looking down over Machu Picchu from the Watchman's Hut, the dry moat and barrier wall that protect the city's southern flank are clearly visible. Beyond them, the city proper is divided into two sections, with a series of grassy plazas in between. This division was partly dictated by topography: the granite spine on which the buildings of Machu Picchu stand rises on either side of the central depression, and Inca architects exploited this natural feature by terracing the sloping sides of the depression and leveling the central square. But there is probably additional significance to this division, for as Cobo explained, the Incas "divided every town or chiefdom into two sections or groups, known as hanan-saya and hurin-saya, which means upper ward and lower ward." The two wards ranked equally, and the separation was partly a device to split the loyalties of the Inca's subjects—a form of insurance against sedition. It also gave the population an incentive for competition in any task they undertook on royal orders: At festivals and public celebrations each ward sought to outdo the other in the inventions and entertainments it devised. Some experts argue that the two halves of Machu Picchu mirrored one another, each saya having its own temples, palace, barracks, school, and convent

for holy women. Other authorities dispute this, assigning a different function to each group of buildings in Machu Picchu and seeing its town plan as haphazard, like a patterned blanket thrown over a great rock and falling in many folds.

From the Watchman's Hut, the most important shrines of Machu Picchu are clearly visible. In the center of the city is a beautiful curving wall. Peruvians call this the *torreón,* or bastion, because of its resemblance to the round tower in a medieval castle. On closer inspection, however, it is clear that there was nothing military about this wall. The Incas normally preferred rectangular plans and right-angled corners in their buildings, and the only examples of curving walls in Inca architecture are those enclosing shrines. The *torreón* at Machu Picchu does just that: its base abuts a grotto that was long ago converted into a holy mausoleum, and its curving length encloses a spur of granite that rises from the mountainside at this point. The top of this spur is enclosed by the parapet of the tower in much the same way that the Dome of the Rock in Jérusalem curves around a holy outcrop of rock. Hiram Bingham called this structure a "sun temple," and the attribution is not unreasonable: the sun temple in Cuzco, whose function is definitely known, also has a curving wall built around an outcrop of rock.

Alongside the upper level of Machu Picchu's *torreón* is a rectangular chamber of the most brilliant Inca masonry, its ashlars cut and fitted with dazzling virtuosity and its row of trapezoidal niches cut with crisp precision. Beyond this is an equally beautiful

two-story house, also of the finest stonework. This lovely building is now known, for no compelling reason, as the House of the Princess. It probably housed the temple priests or provided chapels for the worship of the moon and other celestial bodies. The only problem archaelogists have in designating this important group of structures as a sun temple is that it lacks the six chambers for the associated deities that are normally part of a sun temple. The *torreón* also lacks a tabernacle or niche to hold an image of the sun. The main sun temple in Cuzco had such a golden image, which faced the east so that it would reflect the rays of the rising sun. There are corbels on the eastern and southern faces of the Machu Picchu *torreón,* however, and these might once have supported the image. A more curious feature of the building is a tall, trapezoidal gate that opens onto a void on the north side of the curving tower. The base of this gate is cut in a stepped shape and there are strange holes drilled through the stones on either side of the base. Did these holes once support a sun image? Were they used to carry off sacrificial liquids? Or, according to a more fanciful theory, might they have been used as tunnels for snakes in some divination ritual? Machu Picchu abounds in such enigmas.

The cavern beneath the *torreón* is equally mysterious. Inca masons skillfully converted the hollow beneath the rock outcrop into a chamber. Walls of ashlars rise smoothly out of the bedrock, and an entrance has been formed by cutting the rock into an elegant stepped shape. Bingham called this the "royal mausoleum"; and if it was not a mau-

soleum it was clearly a holy place, for it lies at the heart of the city and was fashioned with the most painstaking effort. The notion that it contained royal mummy bundles may be valid, for we do know that the Incas mummified their rulers and nobles and regularly paraded these richly robed corpses in their ceremonies. One of the most famous of sixteenth-century chroniclers, Garcilaso de la Vega, who was the son of a conquistador and an Inca princess, recalled seeing royal mummies when he was a boy in Cuzco:

> The bodies were so perfect that they lacked neither hair, eyebrows nor eyelashes. They were in clothes such as they had worn when alive, with *llautus* [royal cord diadems] on their heads but no other sign of royalty. They were seated in the way that Indian men and women usually sit, with their arms crossed over their chests, and their eyes cast down.... I remember touching a finger of the hand of the Inca Huayna-Capac. It was hard and rigid like that of a wooden statue. The bodies weighed so little that any Indian could carry them from house to house in his arms or on his shoulders.

The royal mummies of Cuzco were carried out to the main square every day and seated there in order of antiquity. Each dead ruler was attended by male and female servants who offered food and *chicha,* maize beer, to the mummy. (The food was burned in a brazier and the drink poured into a sacrificial font.) It is quite possible that such ceremonies were repeated at Machu Picchu with the

mummified remains of any rulers who died there, or with effigies of the Incas and their ancestors.

Below the *torreón's* mysterious Serpent Gate is another of Machu Picchu's many enigmatic features—a flight of sixteen stone cisterns that once carried water from the highest part of the city to the agricultural terraces below. As would be expected, the stone tanks are beautifully cut. Their purpose is not clear, however, for the drainage holes are so far down the sides that the cisterns cannot have been filled to any great height. They could thus have been used for human ablutions but not for bathing. Bingham believed this line of cisterns to be a residential water supply; he imagined Inca women coming to fill their narrow-necked jars from this stepped communal trough. But there are no such communal watering places at other Inca sites, and quite logically: the Incas had abundant water and were able to channel it to each part of their towns. Here again the best explanation seems to be a religious one. The Incas are known to have venerated springs and water, and this curious flight of stone tanks may have been an expression of that form of worship (while simultaneously serving to drain off sacrificial effluents from temples along its path). Whatever its purpose, the flow of water must have given the town a delightful splashing counterpoint to the thundering of the Urubamba River far below.

The finest of all Machu Picchu's residential enclosures lies just beyond this man-made cascade. Hiram Bingham dubbed this the "King's Group," and it does seem to be a small-scale version of the great royal palaces of Cuzco and other Inca centers. It was, originally, a walled enclosure entered by a monumental trapezoidal door. This gate has as its lintel a single, massive stone cut with characteristic Inca flair. Bingham reasoned that this must have been a royal palace, for "no one but a king could have insisted on having the lintels of his doorways made of solid blocks of granite each weighing three tons." The Incas, as we have noted, had no cranes or lifting tackle, so these cyclopean blocks must have been raised on earth ramps. "What a prodigious amount of patient effort had to be employed!" Bingham marveled.

Although the workmanship and central location of this compound indicate that it may have been a royal residence, it is not large. Inside the gate is a small yard and beyond it a central court flanked by two fine buildings with niches cut into their walls. One of these, with a water channel running into a narrow internal passage, is thought to have been the ruler's sleeping quarters; the other may have been an audience chamber. Beyond are "servants' quarters" executed in rustic masonry; below is an enclosed terrace that may have served as a garden.

It was Garcilaso de la Vega who noted that "all the royal palaces had gardens and orchards for the Inca's recreation. These were planted with all sorts of charming and beautiful trees, beds of flowers and . . . herbs found in Peru. They also made gold and silver replicas of many trees and lesser plants . . . done life size, with all their leaves, blossoms and fruits." When the first invaders encountered the Inca ruler Atahualpa at Cajamarca in northern

Inca masons showed a marked preference for the rectilinear; indeed, the only curved walls in Inca architecture are those enclosing shrines. The center of Machu Picchu is dominated by the torreón, a truncated tower (left) whose shape suggests a military purpose but whose function was exclusively religious. Abutting the base of the torreón is a small grotto that experts believe served, in Inca times, as a mausoleum. Like the larger and more famous Royal Mausoleum (above), once the repository of Machu Picchu's noble dead, it is carved out of living rock, with supplemental stonework added on where needed. Directly adjacent the torreón is an exquisitely constructed two-story structure known as the House of the Princess (far left in the photograph at left). Its upper story has fallen into disrepair, but the lower is splendidly preserved, as habitable today as it was five hundred years ago.

After creating the first men and women in his own image, the sun god Viracocha dispersed them underground with orders to emerge from certain cave mouths and natural springs, and there to found the original settlements of Peru. Among Viracocha's charges were four brothers, known in Inca mythology by the surname Ayar, who made their appearance from a three-mouthed cave near Cuzco. Hiram Bingham was to argue that the windows set into the long wall of Machu Picchu's commanding structure, the so-called Temple of the Three Windows (right), recalled the myth of the brothers Ayar. In any case the imposing façade of the building dominates the ruins that Bingham discovered.

Peru, he received them in a small palace similar to the King's Group at Machu Picchu. Spanish officers described his residence as consisting of four chambers around a central patio. It included a stone bath with hot and cold piped water. The Inca reportedly slept in a room overlooking a walled garden, and the chamber opposite was plastered white and roofed by thatched domes. Two other chambers were for servants.

Those first Spaniards, who had the privilege of observing a reigning Inca, stressed the fine textiles that surrounded him. The Inca sat on a low stool covered in lovely cloth, his chamber was hung with fine tapestries, and a flock of women were in constant attendance on him. The young page Pedro Pizarro recalled this scene vividly:

Ladies brought [the Inca] his meal and placed it before him on tender thin green rushes . . . They placed all his vessels of gold, silver and pottery on these rushes. He pointed to whatever he fancied and it was brought. One of his ladies took it and held it in her hand while he ate. He was eating in this manner one day when I was present. A slice of food was being lifted to his mouth when a drop fell onto the clothing he was wearing. Giving his hand to the Indian lady, he rose and went into his chamber to change his dress and returned wearing a dark brown tunic and cloak. I approached him and felt the cloak, which was softer than silk. I asked him: "Inca, of what is a robe as soft as this made?" . . . He explained that it was from the skins of [vampire] bats that fly by night.

Everything touched by the Inca—including the remains of his meals and even his fingernail parings and trimmed hair—was stored and then carefully destroyed to prevent its being used in witchcraft. Such cautions suggest a divinity bordering on godhead, but for all their power and prodigious wealth the Incas actually lived relatively simply, with little in the way of household goods or furniture. They did not use beds or hammocks, as Pedro Pizarro noted, but "these lords slept on the ground on large cotton mattresses. They had large woolen blankets to cover them."

The holy character of Machu Picchu emerges most strongly in the buildings that rise on a ridge behind the King's Group. This granite outcrop is the dominant feature of the inner city, and every building on it has obvious religious significance. A long staircase leads from the King's Group to the Sacred Plaza at the heart of this religious complex. On the side of the plaza that overlooks the central squares and the lower ward of Machu Picchu is the so-called Temple of the Three Windows. This building has an open side facing the plaza; its other walls are built of large blocks interlocking with a precision that only master masons could achieve. Three large windows look out over the city and the forested mountains beyond. They have the familiar trapezoidal shape, but here it is subtly modified, with rounded lower corners and slightly curved sides. The windows are cut with such exactitude that these variations are clearly intentional.

Hiram Bingham argued, plausibly, that these three windows symbolized the three caves that play an important part in the Incas' origin legend. According to that myth the Inca tribe was founded by four brothers called Ayar, who migrated northward from Lake Titicaca on the edge of what is now the Bolivian altiplano. The brothers traveled underground for most of this distance and emerged near Cuzco from the three mouths of a cave called Tambo-toqo. They then moved on, after various adventures, to settle in the rich mountain valley of Cuzco, where they founded the dynasty of Incas and launched the Inca tribe on the first of its many conquests. The cave of Tambo-toqo was thus of fundamental importance in the cult that surrounded the semi-divine Inca emperor, for it represented a crucial turning point in his ancestors' history—an event venerated in the way Muslims revere Muhammad's Night Journey to Jerusalem. The three windows of this temple at Machu Picchu dominate the city so completely that it is highly likely that they indeed represent the three cave mouths of the origin legend.

Having made this reasonable proposal, Hiram Bingham went further. All the sixteenth-century chroniclers agreed that the cave of Tambo-toqo was at a place called Paccaritambo, which is some 30 miles south of Cuzco on the route between the Incas' capital city and Lake Titicaca. Bingham noted that the Paccaritambo that lay south of Cuzco had few Inca remains, which is surprising for a place of such religious importance. By contrast, Machu Picchu is full of buildings of obvious religious significance. The native chronicler Santacruz Pachacuti Yamqui wrote that the first Inca, Manco Capac, ordered that his people should build at Paccaritambo "masonry with a form of opening, consisting of three windows, that would signify the home of his fathers from whom he was descended." Bingham argued that the Temple of the Three Windows had been built in fulfillment of Manco Capac's order; that Machu Picchu—not Paccaritambo—was the true Tambo-toqo; and thus his discovery was far older than the two-century-old Inca dynasty. "I am convinced," he claimed, "that the name of the older part of Machu Picchu was Tampu-tocco [Tambo-toqo] . . . and that here was the capital of the little kingdom where, during the centuries—possibly eight or ten—[before the Incas], there were kept alive the wisdom, skill, and best traditions of the ancient folk who had developed the civilization of Peru, using agricultural terraces as its base."

This is an intriguing theory. Unfortunately, it does not hold up upon serious consideration. Bingham's own excavations revealed no pre-Inca objects. Moreover, there has been considerable study of Inca architecture and building methods since Bingham's discovery of Machu Picchu in 1911, and there is now no question that all the buildings are of late Inca style. Also, finally, Machu Picchu is *northwest* of Cuzco, far from the route of any tribe migrating north from Lake Titicaca.

Alongside the Temple of the Three Windows is another of Machu Picchu's great temples. This too is a three-sided building with an open side facing the Sacred Plaza, built in monolithic style. The huge boulders fitted into its walls misled Bingham and others into imagining that they were the product

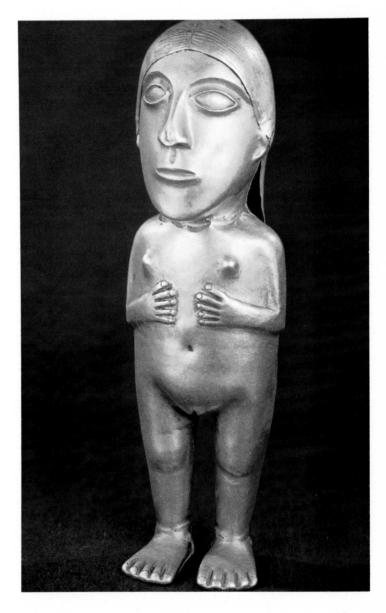

of a pre-Inca people. These mighty stones were in fact the work of the most audacious and flamboyant of the Inca masons, and the great blocks at the base of this temple's walls form the foundation for neat courses of typical Inca ashlars that contain rows of lovely symmetrical niches. At the back of this temple is an enormous altar stone, elegantly cut and fitted into the rear wall. It measures 14 feet long by 4½ feet tall and 3 feet deep. Thought to have been dedicated to Viracocha, the creator god of Inca mythology, this is often called the Principal Temple of the city.

Behind the Principal Temple, a narrow, twisting path and several flights of stairs lead toward the most famous and holiest of all Machu Picchu's shrines. This route, doubtless followed by priests in bygone times, is now used by thousands of modern visitors. The first point of interest on this climb is a small chamber that is perhaps the most perfect of all Machu Picchu's many beautiful buildings. On either side of its single door are stone blocks sunk into the base of the wall. Each of these blocks has no less than thirty-two angles or corners, in three dimensions, all fitting perfectly with the adjoining stones. Inside, Inca masons provided a tour de force demonstration of their virtuosity in the precision and polish of the ashlars, the sharp cut of the niches, and the turning of stones to strengthen the chamber's corners. Hiram Bingham thought that this chamber might have been used to display mummies of Inca notables, and he boasted, justifiably, that in its proportions and beauty this chamber was the equal of any ancient building anywhere. It is known today as the Ornament Chamber.

The path that passes the Ornament Chamber climbs in short flights of steps past clusters of buildings and up several terrace levels to the peak of Machu Picchu's ridge—an appropriately dramatic approach to a holy place. The top of the granite outcrop has been sculpted into a rectangular pinnacle, a stone gnomon rising six feet above its masonry base. This is the so-called *inti-huatana*, or "hitching-post" of the sun. (The word *inti* means "sun"; as a verb *huata* means "to tie.") George Squier, an energetic American traveler who visited much of Peru in the 1870s, was one of the first modern observers to guess at the importance of these stone pinnacles. Squier had seen them in Inca ruins at Huaitará in the central Andes and at Pisac near Cuzco, and he described them as "*inti-huatanas* or sun-fingers, where the sun might appear to be stopped, or tied up for a moment in his course; and on which, in his passage through the zenith, he might sit down in all his glory." Squier would have marveled at Machu Picchu's *inti-huatana*, the highest such gnomon to survive at any Inca site and a masterpiece of sculpture, rising from a tapering base in a single strong upward thrust.

Worship of the sun, the most potent force in the agricultural calendar, was fundamental to Inca religion, as we have noted. Preoccupation with the movements of this prepotent celestial body had turned the Incas into efficient astronomers—not as sophisticated as the Maya or Aztecs, perhaps, but well aware of the movements of the sun and the major stars. In the words of the Peruvian-born

chronicler Felipe Huaman Poma, "They calculated
the month, day, hour and precise moment for sowing their crops, observing the movements of the
sun.... Variations in its direction and intensity acted as a precise clock to regulate the sowing and
harvesting of their foods." Another chronicler, the
half-Inca Garcilaso de la Vega, described how, to
ascertain the time of the equinoxes, the Incas

> had splendidly-carved stone columns erected in the
> courtyards of temples of the sun ... These columns
> stood in the center of great circles that filled the
> courts or open spaces. A line was drawn with a
> cord across the center of the circle ... When the
> shadow at sunrise fell exactly along this line, and
> at midday the sun lit all sides of the column and
> cast no shadow, they knew that that day was the
> equinox. They then decked the columns with all
> the flowers and aromatic herbs they could find, and
> placed the throne of the sun upon it, saying that
> on that day the sun was seated on the column in
> all the fulness of his light.

Worship of the sun culminated in great cermon-
ials called *inti raymi*, or sun festival, held in the
months of June and December. A young Spanish
priest recorded his impressions of such a festival
during the first months of the Spanish occupation
of Cuzco, before Christian clergy had suppressed
such manifestations. He wrote that "the Inca
opened the sacrifices and they lasted for eight days.
Thanks were given to the sun for the past harvest
and prayers were made for the crops to come."

Sacred images from all the shrines of Cuzco were
brought out to a plain at the eastern side of the
city, where they were housed under the avenue of
magnificent featherwork awnings and attended by
the nobility and priesthood, all dressed in splendid
robes and adorned with gold and silver headdresses
and breastplates. "As soon as the sunrise began,
they started to chant in marvellous harmony and
unison. While chanting, each of them shook his
foot, ... and as the sun continued to rise, they
chanted louder," the Inca himself presided over
this elaborate ceremony. There were sacrifices of
llamas and offerings of other foods. At one point
two hundred young girls arrived from the city carrying pitchers of *chicha*. "They also offered to the
sun many bales of a herb that the Indians chew
and call *coca*, whose leaf is like myrtle. There were
many other rituals and sacrifices. Suffice it to say
that when the sun was about to set in the evening,
the Indians showed great sadness at its departure
in their chants and expressions. They allowed their
voices to die away on purpose. And as the sun
was sinking completely and disappearing from sight
they made a great act of reverence, raising their
hands and worshipping it in the deepest humility."

One imagines that kindred ceremonies occurred
at Machu Picchu in its heyday. The crowd of celebrants would have massed in the central squares.
Above them, silhouetted against the setting sun,
would have stood the priests gathered about the
inti-huatana. And, beyond them, the sheer drop to
the Urubamba canyon and the line of mountains
disappearing to the west.

III

Navel of the World

To the Incas, the city of Cuzco was the "navel of the world"—at once a holy place and the heart of their great empire. The capital city was so important that the domain of the Incas could well have been called the Cuzcano empire, much as we refer to the Roman empire. In fact, when the first Spaniards arrived in northern Peru, that ragtag band of adventurers led by Francisco Pizarro were to hear so much about Cuzco from the Indian tribesmen they encountered that they initially confused its name with that of the Inca ruler himself.

Ironically, when the Spanish conquistadores finally marched into the Inca capital in November 1533, they were, at first, slightly disappointed. Anyone approaching Cuzco from the northwest emerges onto a plateau above the low hills that overlook the city in that direction. The city is suddenly spread out below: nestled on the slope of a hill at the edge of a grassy valley 11,000 feet above sea level. In Inca times its houses were all roofed in gray thatch, and smoke from hundreds of wood or peat fires would have hung over these steeply pitched roofs. Most of the houses were single-story, and those on the edges of the city were simple rectangles with walls of adobe bricks set on a stone base. The roofs rested on beams of agave, a cactus-like tree, and the thatch was tough *ichu* grass, tied down with creepers to stone bosses sunk into the gables of the house walls. Most roofs had wide eaves to shelter passers-by from the heavy mountain rains. Pedro Sancho, who was Francisco Pizarro's secretary, recalled that "most of [Cuzco's] buildings are of stone and the rest have half their façade of stone. There are also many adobe houses, very efficiently made, which are arranged along straight streets on a grid plan. The streets are all paved, with a stone-lined water channel running down the middle of each street. Their only fault is to be narrow: only one mounted man can ride on either side of the channel."

It was only at its center that Cuzco took on the appearance of a great capital. The heart of the city lay on a triangular slope between two mountain streams, and all of Cuzco's monumental buildings were found there. The Peruvians perceived their metropolis as a crouching puma, a mountain lion whose head was a mighty temple-fortress atop a cliff overlooking the central city. The zigzag ramparts of this fortress represented the feline's teeth. The puma's body was considered the slope between the streams, an area of palaces and temples whose ceremonial square was held to represent the animal's heart. The triangular district where the streams joined was known as *puma-chupan*, or the "puma's tail."

Cuzco was an especially clean and healthy city, set as it is in the cool, clear air of the high Andes. In the early 1440s the great Inca Pachacuti had drained the outlying marshes while rebuilding his tribal home. He also razed the city's peasant huts to make room for later palaces. The streams—the Huatanay and Tullumayo—were efficiently enclosed in stone-lined channels at this same time; the chronicler Pedro de Cieza de León said that "in the days of the Incas, the Huatanay was very clean with its water running over stones. At times the Incas went

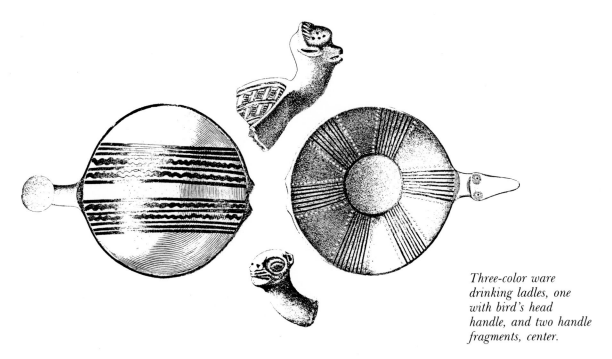

Three-color ware drinking ladles, one with bird's head handle, and two handle fragments, center.

to bathe there with their women." One of these streams flowed in its channel between the two vast squares that formed the setting for all important Inca ceremonies. To the west lay Cusipata, the square of entertainment, where the common people crowded to celebrate their festivals. To the east was the larger Aucaypata, surrounded on three sides by magnificent Inca palaces and temples. Both squares were surfaced with a deep layer of fine gravel.

The first Spaniards to reach Cuzco observed an Inca coronation ceremony in Aucaypata square. An eyewitness recalled that "such a vast number of people assembled every day that they could only crowd onto the square with great difficulty." The mummified bodies of dead Incas played a prominent part in such jubilations:

There was a litter for each one, with men in its livery to carry it. The natives came down in this way, singing many ballads and giving thanks to the sun ... They reached the square accompanied by innumerable people and carrying the Inca at their head in his litter.... The dead kings were seated on their thrones and surrounded by pages and women with flywhisks in their hands, who ministered to them with as much respect as if they had been alive.... There were so many people, and both men and women were such heavy drinkers, and they poured so much into their skins—for their entire activity was drinking, not eating—that it is a fact that two wide drains over eighteen inches in diameter which emptied into the river beneath the flagstones ... ran with urine throughout the day, from those who urinated into them, as abundantly as a flowing spring. This was not remarkable when one considers the amount they were drinking and the numbers drinking it. But the sight was a marvel and something never seen before!

The cult of ancestor worship had become a serious drain on the Inca state by the time of the Conquest, for as the chronicler Cobo explained, "When the king died, his prince did not inherit his palace and fortune: it was left, together with the body of the deceased, to the clan he had founded. The entire estate was dedicated to the cult of his body and the support of his descendants. The clan embalmed the body of its royal father and preserved it together with all its belongings and ornaments." Even in death Inca rulers held sway over the living, "governing" estates maintained by vast staffs of servants in all parts of Peru. In time most of the best agricultural land was held by such legacies. As Pedro Pizarro noted, the dead Incas were "served in death as well as they had been in life. Their service of gold and silver was not touched, nor was anything else which they had owned; those who served in their palaces were retained and replaced, and provinces were set aside to support them." One Inca ruler did attempt to abolish this wasteful custom, declaring that the dead "had all that was best in his kingdom"—but even he failed to break the power of his forebears' clans.

The most obvious manifestation of each of these dead dynasts was his palace in Cuzco, which was

The eventful history of Cuzco, one-time capital of the Inca empire, is chronicled in stone, and can be read, by the practiced eye, in virtually any quadrant of the city. From the air Cuzco is a distinctly Spanish metropolis of red tile roofs and baroque basilicas (lower left); from the ground, Cuzco reveals a more complex paternity. The valley in which it sits was settled in 1438 by a young Inca prince named Pachacuti. Over the next century the Incas were to lay out a vast new city of radiating thoroughfares, and broad plazas. The Spanish, whose talents were military, not masonic, simply built upon the foundations laid by their predecessors—and Cuzco's colonial structures (opposite) often rest on bases of Inca stonework.

kept intact, sometimes for generations after his death, and remained the repository of the dead man's possessions. His mummy was housed there, seated on his quondam throne, wrapped in layers of magnificent cloth, and adorned with gold. It was venerated as in life, and was carried out into Cuzco's central square for daily rituals. This practice put the royal treasures of Cuzco on daily display, but the Incas were so sure of the security of their empire and the loyalty of their subjects that they felt no need to hide or bury their treasures. The Spanish conquistadores were another matter, however: they looted Cuzco with unexampled rapacity, picking clean the mausoleum-mansions of former Inca rulers as well as the treasuries of the living. As a consequence, there is no likelihood of an archaeological find in Peru equivalent to the discovery of Tutankamen's tomb in Egypt or the great burial mounds of China.

Even Pizarro's secretary, a pedantic Spanish official, was impressed by central Cuzco. He wrote to his king that "the city of Cuzco . . . is large and beautiful enough to be remarkable even in Spain. It is full of the palaces of nobles, for no poor people live there. Each ruler builds himself a palace, and so do all the chiefs." The palaces of four rulers surrounded the square, he observed, and these he described as "the most important buildings in the city, built of ashlars and painted. The finest palace is that of the last Inca, Huayna Capac. It has a gateway of red, white and multicolored marble, and has other flat-roofed structures that are also most remarkable."

This particular palace, Amaru-cancha, or Court of the Snake, stood on the south side of the square, on the site now occupied by the Jesuits' beautiful baroque church. The Court of the Snake was demolished soon after the Spaniards conquered Cuzco, and Garcilaso de la Vega remembered that when he was a boy—in the 1550s—all that remained of Amaru-cancha was a fine round tower. This tower's stone walls were four times the height of a man, "but its roof, made of excellent timber they used for their royal palaces, was so high that I could say without exaggeration that it equalled in height any tower in Spain, apart from [the Giralda] in Seville. Its roof was rounded like the walls, and above it, in place of a weathervane, . . . it had a very tall, thick pole that enhanced its height and beauty."

Opposite Amaru-cancha was Cassana, the palace of the great conqueror Pachacuti. This building had an ornamental gateway inlaid with silver and flanked by two round towers built of fine masonry and roofed in skillfully laid thatch. The greatest glory of the Cassana palace was its vast baronial hall—a feature typical of Inca palaces. Many had large halls, some of them up to 200 yards long and 50 to 60 yards wide. They were unpartitioned and served as places of assembly for festivals and dances in inclement weather. The largest of these halls was that of Cassana, which could hold three thousand people. Indeed, the very name Cassana meant "something to freeze"—because, as Garcilaso de la Vega explained, "its buildings were so large and splendid" that anyone seeing them was frozen with wonderment.

Garcilaso's claim may seem exaggerated, but it is confirmed by other chroniclers. The palace of Cassana has been destroyed, but foundations of similar great halls, known as *kallanka*, survive in other Inca ruins. Two such halls, at Huánuco in central Peru, are each 230 feet long, and another, in eastern Bolivia, encloses a floor measuring 256 feet long by 85 feet wide. Careful study of these and other ruins has revealed how the Incas roofed their huge assembly halls: They used rows of wooden pillars—or, less often, a central retaining wall—to support a trellis of roof beams. These in turn held a lattice onto which the thatch was fastened. Some *kallanka* have a series of portals along one of their long walls, with the short walls rising to pointed gables. Pedro Pizarro indicated that Cassana's great hall was of different design, however. It was "very long, with the entrance at one end, so that everything inside could be seen from it. This entrance was so large that it stretched from wall to wall and was all open to the roof line."

An Inca palace, like any true palace, was more than a mere residence. Its outer precincts served as both base and barracks for the royal bodyguard, and its outbuildings as administrative offices. According to the Indian chronicler Huaman Poma, there were also special buildings for the reception of visitors, a dormitory for tributary labor and personal servants, areas for storage, a brewery for the preparation of *chicha,* and accommodations for the poor. Certain inner rooms of the palace could be visited only by senior officials, most of whom were blood relatives of the Inca. The inner chambers,

der, the rainbow, the planet Venus and the other where the Inca resided, were hung with fine textiles and included living quarters for the Inca's female attendants. In the words of Martín de Murúa, "All this was full of delights, for they had various arbors and gardens, and the lodgings were very large and worked with marvelous skill."

Two blocks south of Cuzco's main square was the empire's most venerated sanctuary, the sun temple Coricancha. This was the most sumptuous and most important temple in the empire, and Jesuit chronicler Cobo could only compare it to the fountainhead of his own religion—Rome. "It was considered the head and metropolitan temple of their false religion," he later observed, "and was the holiest sanctuary of these Indians. All the people of the Inca empire frequented it, coming on pilgrimages out of piety. It was called Coricancha, which means 'Enclosure of Gold,' because of the incomparable wealth of this metal that was buried among its chapels and on its walls, vaults and altars. It was dedicated to the Sun, although statues of Viracocha, the Thunder, Moon and other leading idols were also placed in it; for it served the same purpose as the Pantheon in Rome."

As with many Inca buildings, the plan of Coricancha is deceptively simple. It consists of six chambers arranged around a large square courtyard. Each chamber is a simple rectangle, each with doors opening onto the courtyard but otherwise unconnected to other parts of the temple. The six chambers were once separate chapels, five dedicated to the main celestial deities—the sun, the moon, thun-

stars—with the sixth reserved for the high priest.

Fortunately for modern archaeologists and visitors, Coricancha passed into the hands of the Dominican monastic order soon after the Spanish Conquest—and they have occupied the site ever since. The Dominicans were well aware that Coricancha was the most holy place in the Inca empire, and they scrupulously maintained it as a church and monastery. Its courtyard plan was easily adaptable to their notion of a cloister, making it possible to build baroque arcades above the temple's chambers without destroying the original Inca walls. Cuzco was shaken by a severe earthquake in May 1950, and the Spanish colonial-period buildings of the Dominican church were badly damaged. The tremor also revealed hidden stretches of Inca walling—far better built and far more durable than the later additions—and since 1950 a team of Peruvian restorers has been trying to reconcile the mixture of Inca and colonial walls in this historic building. They have, for the interim, propped up the colonial arcades on makeshift scaffolding, and they have boldly rebuilt missing stretches of the Inca walls in imitation of the supposed original.

The simplicity of Coricancha's plan was more than compensated for by the splendor of its stonework. To an early observer, the masonry of this great temple represented the apogee of Inca craftsmanship. Inside and out the temple was constructed of amazing ashlars, set skillfully, "without mortar, and so finely adjusted that it would be impossible to improve on them." Another chronicler compared Coricancha to the most famous buildings

in Spain—and admitted that it exceeded them in terms of its walls and the cutting and laying of its stones. There is, for instance, a magnificent stretch of wall along the eastern side of the temple. Its blocks fit with uncanny precision, and the bulge on the surface of each block is brilliantly controlled. The most famous wall of Coricancha is a curving terrace wall of black andesite that runs beneath the western end of the colonial church. Inca masons customarily built such walls to incline slightly inward—and then created a faint bulge halfway up the wall to create an optical illusion of verticality.

The feature of Coricancha that most excited the Spaniards was not its masonry but its gold, of course. The temple was surrounded by a cornice of gold fastened to the stone. More, "these buildings were sheathed in gold, in large plates, on the side where the sun rises," wrote one eyewitness, adding that the more the buildings were shaded from the sun, the baser the gold they had on them. These plates were removed by the European vandals, yielding a total of seven hundred plates that looked "like boards from chests ... with holes where they had been nailed." Each weighed 4½ pounds—72 ounces of pure gold.

Coricancha also contained a famous image of the rising sun—which the natives managed to hide from the conquerors. One source holds that it was an idol of solid gold, shaped like a year-old baby and dressed in the finest clothing; another, that it was "an image of the sun of great size, made of gold, beautifully wrought and set with many precious stones." Whatever its appearance, this sun image

was taken in religious procession to the main square of Cuzio every morning. The high priest and other attendants accompanied the idol into the square, where the golden sun was placed on a platform covered in bright feather work. Offerings of *chicha* and food were made to it. While the attendants were burning these offerings an Indian would cry out so that all could hear. At his call "everyone who was in the square or outside it crouched down and fell silent, without speaking, coughing or moving, until the food was consumed."

Holy women served an important function in the Inca religion, and the sun temple had a complement of such women, who attended the sun image while it rested on its gold-plated platform during the day and who slept alongside it in a golden chamber at night. "These were daughters of the nobility and claimed to be wives of the sun, pretending that the sun made love to them," says the cynical Pedro Pizarro. "They pretended to live chastely, but they lied, for they involved themselves with the male servants and guardians of the Sun, who were many." These holy women also tended a famous garden of maize that grew alongside the temple, and at certain important festivals they filled this garden with stalks of maize made of gold and surmounted by life-sized cobs and leaves, all of fine gold. One of these beautiful golden plants, a masterpiece of Inca gold work, was taken back to Spain to be shown to the Emperor Charles V. But the emperor, for all that he was a patron of Titian and other Renaissance artists, would not deign even to look at this priceless object. He ordered his officials to

Not quite Vestal Virgins, yet not really members of the Inca's harem either, the mamaconas, *or "chosen women" of Inca society, served as the most personal of personal attendants upon their liege lord. Regarded with envy by the well-born and with the sort of reverence accorded holy women by the peasantry, the members of this elect sorority wove cloth for the Inca's use (right), prepared all his meals, brewed his maize beer, and even attended to his wife's elaborate personal toilette (left).*

place it and other Inca treasures on public display for a few weeks—and then to melt them down.

It was the custom of the Inca rulers to regard a full sister as their most legitimate queen. A few hundred of the female members of the vast imperial family were also reserved for the Inca's pleasure, and these royal concubines were in turn served by contingents of girls from all parts of Peru, selected for their court posts on the basis of their beauty. Every important Inca town had an *aclla-huasi*, "convent," of these *mamaconas*, or chosen women. Their sole occupations were to weave cloth for the Inca, of a quality superior to taffeta or silk; to prepare a special, rich *chicha*, matured for a month; and to make agreeable meals for the Inca.

These convents of women were also an important prop of Inca rule, for the beautiful cloth they wove was an essential item of barter and reward. Part of the Inca's prestige and wealth derived from his huge stocks of such cloths, which he was able to dispense to subject chiefs or deserving officials. The *chicha* and food the chosen women prepared also helped to enhance the Inca's authority, for the emperor kept his subjects happy with regular festivals, as emperors will. Cieza de León described the Hatun Raimi, or Solemn Feast, which was one of the celebrations that marked the annual corn and potato harvest, as lasting for fifteen or twenty days, during which there were great *taquis*, or drinking feasts, and other celebrations, in the course of which llamas, guinea pigs, and pigeons were sacrificed. "The *mamaconas* came forth richly attired and with a great quantity of *chicha*, which they considered sacred . . .

After the men had eaten and drunk repeatedly and were all drunk, including the Inca and the High Priest, joyful and warmed by the liquor, they assembled shortly after midday and started singing in a loud voice songs and ballads that had been composed by their ancestors."

Other chroniclers were to describe how the chosen women prepared hundreds of maize cakes for these festivities: "The flour for this bread . . . was ground and kneaded by the chosen virgins, the 'wives of the Sun,' who also prepared the rest of the food for the feast. The banquet symbolized a gift from the Sun to his children . . . and for that reason the virgins, as wives of the Sun, prepared it." But it was the Incas, as semi-divine rulers closely involved in the official religion, who gained most by these great celebrations. "They made the people joyful, giving them solemn banquets and drinking feasts, great *taquis* and other celebrations, in their manner which is completely different from ours. In these the Incas demonstrate their splendor. All the feasting is at their expense."

Quite apart from their value in making cloth and preparing drink and food, the chosen women had sexual value, providing the Inca, his senior officials, and his generals with a harem. According to Pedro Pizarro, the Inca slept with his sister-queens for a week at a time, in rotation. Each of these important ladies arrived with her complement of *acllas*, or serving girls, and during the appointed week "either she slept with him herself or her Indian girl who pleased him most did so." To supply this royal harem a search for beautiful girls was con-

Because the Incas held that gold belonged to the gods—and so was above commerce—bolts of fine cloth were the medium of exchange in the Inca empire. From their predecessors the Incas inherited a tradition of textile-making that was unequalled in its variety and excellence by that of any other civilization. They employed every known technique, from tapestry to tie-dye, and they exploited every imaginable material, incorporating shells, beads, beaten gold, and iridescent feathers into their fabrics. The results were always striking (right), and often strikingly contemporary—an observation that applies with equal force to the products of modern Inca looms (opposite and below).

ducted by royal officials throughout the empire. It was considered an honor for a girl to be chosen to serve the Inca in this way, and in provincial cities young girls who held promise of adult beauty were groomed as *mamaconas*. The Inca would give some of these women, those he did not keep for himself, to Indians he chose to honor. The girls thus became a kind of royal bounty.

Girls and women reserved for the service of the Inca and the official religion were, naturally, carefully protected, living in well-guarded enclosures and well-supplied with food and luxuries. The *aclla-huasi* of Cuzco lay directly between the sun temple Coricancha and the main square. Daily processions of priests bearing the sun image passed along a beautiful lane between the superb stone walls of the Amaru-cancha palace and the *aclla-huasi*. This street is still intact. By coincidence, the *aclla-huasi* itself passed, soon after the Conquest, into the hands of an order of Catholic nuns, just as the sun temple was acquired by the Dominican friars. The nuns have maintained the harem compound ever since the sixteenth century; as a result, its Inca remains have not been fully explored by archaeologists, but this continuous occupation by modern holy women has ensured the survival of much of the original building.

Where the *aclla-huasi* faces the main square, recent cleaning has revealed a rounded corner with Inca ashlars, cut with consummate skill, that bulge with elegant rustication. The wall as a whole inclines slightly inward for greater strength, and each successive course of stones is smaller than the one below. A modern visitor approaching the square from Coricancha looks past the beautiful corner of the *aclla-huasi* through a colonial colonnade to the handsome Spanish baroque cathedral built on the site of the Inca temple to Viracocha—and, beyond it, to the houses of upper Cuzco, climbing the slope of the hill between the two streams. At the top of this hill is the mighty temple-fortress of Sacsayhuaman—the head of the puma in the Incas' conception of their capital city.

It was the great conquering Inca, Pachacuti, who built Sacsayhuaman. Most sixteenth-century Spaniards referred to the building as a fortress, but it was more than that. Cieza de León, for one, properly noted that "as the power of the Incas was increasing and Pachacuti had such great ambitions, . . . he decided to build a temple of the sun which would surpass everything done until then." The work was conceived on such a vast scale that even if the monarchy had lasted another twenty years it could not have been completed. Perhaps sensing this, Pachacuti ordered that twenty thousand men be sent from the provinces and that local villages supply them with food. These great levies were the secret behind the building of so stupendous a monument: "Four thousand of them quarried and cut the stones; six thousand hauled these with great cables of leather and hemp; others dug the ditch and laid the foundations; while still others cut poles and beams for the timbers. . . . Living rock was excavated for the foundations. . . ."

In the time of the Incas, Sacsayhuaman boasted three mighty towers that overlooked the city below.

Pizarro's secretary, who saw them in all their glory, described Sacsayhuaman as a magnificent stone and earth fortress with great embrasures overlooking the city. There were many buildings within the fortress, and one principal tower at the center. This was square, with four or five stories stepped above one another. The rooms and chambers inside were small, but the stones with which they were built were excellently cut. The blocks were so smooth, Pedro Sancho recorded, "that they look like polished slabs; and the courses are regular, as in Spain, with the joints alternating." A leader of a victorious army, Sancho quite naturally viewed Sacsayhuaman with a soldier's eye: "The fortress has too many rooms and towers for one person to visit them all. Many Spaniards who have visited it and who have traveled in Lombardy and other foreign countries, say that they have never seen a building to compare with this fortress nor a stronger castle. It could contain five thousand Spaniards. It could not be battered and it could not be mined, for it is situated at the top of a hill."

Garcilaso de la Vega, half Inca, half Spanish, played in the ruins of Sacsayhuaman as a boy, and he recalled its extraordinary subterranean passages:

The towers went as far below ground as they did above it. There were tunnels between them so that one could pass from one to the others below ground as well as above it.... There were so many underground passages, large and small, twisting and turning in all directions, with so many doors, all of the same size but some opening to one side and some to the other, that anyone entering the maze soon lost his way...When I was a boy, I often went up to the fortress with others of my own age, ... but we never dared enter certain parts of the remaining vaults, except as far as the light of the sun penetrated, lest we should get lost inside.

Sacsayhuaman's three towers rested on a hilltop buttressed by three long terrace-walls, and it is these terraces that astound the modern visitor. They contain some of the largest blocks of stone ever incorporated into any building anywhere in the world. One huge block is calculated to weigh 90 tons, another 128 tons. One single monolithic stone measures 16 feet high by 15½ feet wide by 8½ feet deep. Pedro Sancho, one of the first Europeans to see these walls, exclaimed that "these ramparts are the most beautiful thing to be seen among the buildings of that land. They are built of stones so large that anyone seeing them would say that they cannot have been placed there by human hands. They are as big as the trunks of trees of the forest."

What is even more striking than the size of Sacsayhuaman's boulders is that they are cut and fitted into a perfect polygonal pattern. Each gigantic stone interlocks precisely with its neighbors, and each has an outer surface smoothed into the slight bulge so typical of Inca architecture. One Jesuit chronicler echoed the feelings of all visitors confronting these superb walls for the first time: "It is beyond the power of imagination to understand how these Indians, unaware of machines, engines or implements, could have cut, dressed, raised and lowered great

The Incas laid out Cuzco in the shape of a puma, with the hilltop fortress of Sacsayhuaman as its head. The walls of that redoubt (right), which are serrated like teeth, contain stones that flabbergasted the conquistadores. "It baffles the mind," one wrote, "how they could be brought up and set in place." In truth there was nothing baffling about Sacsayhuaman, which was the result not of engineering sleight of hand but of back-breaking toil: 20,000 Inca conscripts labored for three decades on its mighty maw, some of whose "teeth" weigh upwards of 100 tons.

rocks more like hunks of mountain than building stones, and set them so exactly in their places."

The terraced ramparts of Sacsayhuaman enclose the hillside for a distance of over 400 yards, and they are arranged in mighty zigzags, with some fifty salient and re-entrant angles. This pattern may indeed have been intended to represent the teeth of the Cuzco puma, but it was also an admirable defensive device, for any attacker was always exposed to defenders on his flank. Three terrace walls are all that survive of this triumph of Inca building; they hug the hillside like the gray armor-plating of some vast, landlocked battleship. The towers, chambers, and temple buildings described by the chroniclers are gone, all but their foundations, which were excavated by Peruvian archaeologists in the 1930s. The Spaniards who built houses in sixteenth-century Cuzco were allowed to plunder this monument for building blocks, and they pulled down all the smooth masonry in the walls to save themselves the expense, effort, and delay of having Indians work the stone. The large slabs that formed the roofs of underground passages were taken to serve as lintels and doorways, and smaller stones were used for foundations and walls. In this way the majesty of the temple-fortress was dismantled, bit by bit—and Pedro de Cieza de León, for one, exploded with fury: "I hate to think of the responsibility of those governors who allowed so extraordinary a thing to have been destroyed and cast down, without giving thought to the future! The remains of this fortress . . . should have been preserved in memory of the greatness of this land!"

IV

Peru Before the Incas

The Incas have aptly been compared to the Romans. Both these warrior tribes excelled as soldiers, as engineers, and as administrators, and both are known more for practical achievement than artistic expression. The Romans derived much of their cultural life from Greek and even Egyptian antecedents, and the Incas likewise borrowed many of the refinements of their society from earlier civilizations. They did not hesitate to adopt artistic styles, patterns, and manufacturing techniques from the tribes they conquered or assimilated into their empire, often absorbing the artists and craftsmen who created them as well. The Incas were an austere mountain people, and they were dazzled and sometimes shocked by the older, richer, and more decadent societies of the coastal plains. Having few luxuries themselves—and no particular proclivities for inventing them—the Incas were content merely to imitate these more sybaritic peoples.

Because the Incas were in control of Peru and the central Andes at the time of the Spanish Conquest, and because they were ascendant in that period, an energetic and expansionist tribe, the name Inca has eclipsed those of all the earlier civilizations of Peru. The Incas wanted it that way, and they actively imposed their language, Quechua, throughout their empire. They also maintained a corps of professional historians who recorded official Inca history—verbally, since no peoples in South America had invented writing—and these bards carefully omitted from their rote record all historical events that antedated the advent of the Incas. They were exclusively concerned with the glories of the em-

peror, with the official religion, and the triumphs of Inca armies. Anything that happened before the rise of the Incas was therefore thought of as prehistory; as a result, most of what we know of pre-Inca cultures we have learned from archaeologists.

Fortunately, Peru is rich in archaeological treasures, and there is plenty of material from which to draw conclusions. The narrow coastal plain of Peru is intensely dry, trapped as it is between the high Andes and the Pacific Ocean, whose waters at this point are very cold thanks to the Humbolt Current, which sweeps inshore off Peru. The result of these phenomena is a dearth of precipitation: it virtually never rains on the coastal plain, for those rain clouds that do not discharge their contents on the mountains are swept out over the Pacific by the climatic conditions. However, the coastal plain is watered by frequent rivers from the nearby Andes, and its valleys are very fertile. Moreover, the sea is teeming with fish, and the climate is warm and dry throughout the year. In short, a perfect place for primitive human beings—and a perfect place for preserving the archaeological artifacts they left behind.

The original inhabitants of Peru arrived several thousand years ago. Their earliest known relics are so-called flake choppers, found in a cave in the Peruvian Andes alongside the bones of deer and an extinct type of sloth. These first Peruvians, who apparently had not yet developed stone arrowheads or spear points, migrated south from North America through Mexico and Panama. They were descendants of the very earliest Americans, Central Asians

70

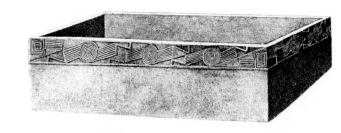

Rectangular stone dishes—the larger 8 inches long—restored from fragments.

who reached Alaska from Siberia during the Ice Ages. During those gelid millennia, the seas were significantly lower and the shallow Bering Strait was exposed, forming a land bridge hundreds of miles wide between Asia and North America. The first movements of human beings along this route could have occurred as early as 23,000 years ago, but significant migration did not begin until the last Ice Age, some 10,000 years ago.

The reason for setting down this capsule history of the origins of the people who settled prehistoric Peru is to dispel the host of spurious theories that have been advanced in this century and the last—all suggesting that the pre-Columbian civilizations of the New World were influenced by some outside force. This "outside force" has been variously identified as Egyptian, Viking, Chinese—even extraterrestial. All have proponents; none has substantiating evidence. Archaeologists have demonstrated a regular cultural progression from the earliest arrivals in Peru to the sophisticated cultures overthrown by the Spaniards in the sixteenth century, and it is their conclusion that there was little if any foreign contact or stimulus during this evolution. If there was a chance arrival of an Asian ship, its crew certainly made little impact on the native civilizations, failing, among other things, to impart such important foreign ideas as writing, the wheel, or the keystone arch.

Archaeological excavations in this century have revealed how early humans progressed in Peru. The most ancient sites, along the coast, are often mere shell middens—great mounds of shells from the

mussels and crustaceans eaten by primitive communities. These middens sometimes contained sharpened stone tools and hunting weapons as well. From about 5000 B.C. there is clear evidence of the cultivation of gourds, beans, and cotton, and mortars can be found in village refuse sites—mortars being sure archaeological evidence of food preparation. In succeeding millennia we see the introduction of fishing nets, fish hooks made of shell, bone scrapers, beads, and organized burial sites with cloth mats and shrouds.

It was in the second millennium B.C. that three major advances occurred: the advent of pottery-making, the cultivation of food crops such as maize, and the rudiments of stone architecture. Most Peruvians of this period lived in shelters or huts of adobe or woven wattle, but a recent excavation near Lima airport has revealed the earliest known stone wall dating from this period—roughly shaped stones that form the corner of a building or terrace.

Around 800 B.C. another remarkable advance in Peruvian cultural evolution was to occur. In a small, obscure mountain valley in the high Cordillera Blanca north of Lima, a Peruvian tribe built a temple complex of amazing sophistication. The remains of this temple are known today simply by a place name—Chavín de Huántar—for, as with almost all pre-Inca cultures, we have no idea of the builders' tribal name. None of the region's preceding cultures had given any indication that early Peruvians were capable of building, designing, and decorating with the advanced skills demonstrated at Chavín; yet, this great temple, far from any town, modern or

72

ancient, was clearly created by a well-organized society with elaborate religious and social structures.

Although the ruins of Chavín were known to many nineteenth-century travelers, its identification as the mother site of a civilization of great antiquity was made in the twentieth century by one of the first Peruvian-born archaeologists to investigate his country's past. Julio C. Tello, who had the added distinction of being of pure Indian blood, studied Chavín and its culture from 1919 onward, during a long and distinguished career. When Tello first proposed that Chavín was built about 500 B.C. — long *before* most of the monuments of classical Greece—his claim was either disputed or ridiculed. It took repeated excavations in northern Peru to establish that the Chavín style had spread over an extensive area, and that it consistently antedated other cultures. It is only with modern carbon and thermo-luminescent dating techniques that Tello's theories have been fully vindicated. If anything, Chavín is now thought to be even older than Tello once supposed it to be.

The main temple of Chavín consists of a central rectangular block with two projecting wings. The southern wing, which has been enlarged three times, is now the most conspicuous feature of the site. It looks like an enormous platform, but it is in fact a windowless building with passages and chambers at three levels. The interior plan is complex, with a labyrinth of chambers, stairs, ramps, and ventilation shafts. In one chamber, deep inside the building, Tello found a magnificent 15-foot-high carved monolith, far too large to have been brought in through the surrounding passages.

The most remarkable feature of this temple, predictably enough, is the quality of its masonry: the walls are alternating courses of large and small dressed stones, cut with a precision almost equal to that achieved by the Incas 2,000 years later. Internal doors and passages are roofed with neat rows of stone lintels, and the large bosses projecting from the outside wall are carved as fierce feline or human heads. Above these ran a carved frieze. The south face of the building is approached by three flights of stairs, the central having a limestone and granite portal. Flanking the base of the staircase is another innovative architectural feature: stone columns, each carved with a bird in low relief. Alongside the temple, and sloping toward its modest mountain valley, are sunken courts and further platforms.

The powerful and distinctive Chavín decorative style spread throughout the northern coastal area and the mountains of Peru during the centuries of Chavín ascendancy. The favored technique is plain incision—sharp, bold lines cut into hard stone or heavy black pottery. The patterns are often cursive or convoluted, with a few standard themes recurring in an elaborate intertwining: among them, jaws with prominent feline fangs, pairs of nostrils, and profile heads of poisonous snakes. Another Chavín hallmark is the "eccentric eye"—a stylized eye, either round or squared, in which the pupil is always in the upper center, as if raised balefully toward heaven.

The most famous Chavín relic is the so-called Raimondi stele, a slab of hard black rock incised with the figure of a god or priest. The figure is seen from the front, legs apart, holding an enormous, elaborate staff in either hand. It wears a six-tiered headdress, and the figure is covered in a baroque pattern of dozens of snakes' heads, feline fangs, jaguar eyes, and nostrils.

Chavín represents the first of the three "horizon" styles that occur in Peruvian archaeology. "Horizon" in this context means a style that managed to spread beyond one or two tribes or valleys, gradually extending its influence over a large part of the country. Symbols of the Chavín style can be identified on pottery found all along the coast of northern Peru and far inland—and there are at least eight temples exhibiting Chavín influence.

The problem for archaeologists has been to determine, if possible, the genesis of this extraordinary culture. Julio Tello thought that it probably originated in the Amazon basin and spread westward from the jungles to the Pacific coast: Chavín itself is located in a valley that connects the two geographical zones of Peru; and Kotosh, another important site with Chavín elements, lies on the Amazon side of Chavín. One group of theorists has argued that Chavín reflects the influence of Mexico, however, and not the Amazon basin. They note that maize cultivation reached the Andes from Central America at about this time, and they see stylistic similarities between the Chavín and Mexican Olmec cultures. But the geographical distance between the two early cultures is actually vast, and there is no indication of any similar styles anywhere in the thousands of miles that lie between Mexico

and Peru. Also, Chavín is several centuries older than Olmec. The most likely explanation, therefore, is that the Chavín style developed locally, in isolation from the rest of the world, and spread from the rich coastal valleys across the mountains—toward the Amazon. Whatever their origin, the builders of Chavín can fairly be said to have made a dramatic cultural advance. They progressed far beyond the tribal societies of their South American contemporaries, and in so doing they laid the foundation for the succession of advanced civilizations that inhabited pre-Conquest Peru.

One clue to the origin of Chavín may lie in another mysterious and fascinating ruin, located on Peru's coastal littoral not far west of the mountain temple. This ruin, called Sechín, lies a few miles south of the port city of Casma. After studying a row of carved and sculpted stone slabs that rose above the sand near the base of a dry, rocky outcrop, Julio Tello rightly concluded that they were of similar antiquity to those found at Chavín. In recent years, further excavations have exposed hundreds more of these sculpted stones, which once decorated the sides of a rectangular platform enclosing an even more ancient mud-brick temple. Sechín's sculptures, cut in low relief with figures of almost life size, are among the most vivid, naturalistic, and dynamic to be found in Peru. Some depict triumphant warriors in strange helmets and armor; others show their naked, defeated victims, often decapitated or dismembered, with entrails hanging from their stomachs or blood spurting from their eye sockets. Some stones have overall patterns

The objects created by Moche artisans were most often made of clay, not the gold favored by their Chavín predecessors, but these polychrome pots are more precious to us today than any precious metal because their extraordinary range of subject matter and realistic detail provide us with a graphic picture of everyday life in ancient Peru. The sheer variety of Moche ware is staggering, including as it does everything from life-like portrait heads (below) to such imaginative creations as the stirrup pot (left, below), which depicts a royal audience convened on an Andean mountaintop. No subject was held to be outside the Moche potter's purview. A puma's attack on an Indian peasant warranted depiction (left), and so did literally every aspect of human sexual behavior.

75

of anatomical details—piles of bones, eyeballs, or vertebrae doubtless intended to represent those plucked from hapless victims.

Sechín was obviously a temple of war or a monument commemorating a great victory, and it is thought to be slightly older than Chavín. Some observers have seen similarities between the sculptures at Sechín and the famous *danzantes*, the rocks of similar size, sculpted with "dancing" figures in low relief, that are found at Monte Albán near Oaxaca in central Mexico. These resemblances are superficial, however, and more easily attributed to coincidence than to cross-cultural influence. Here again the distance between the two sites is immense, and there is no trace of other cultural links to be found anywhere in between. Moreover, it is now established that Sechín is far older than the Zapotec culture that built Monte Albán.

After the flowering of Chavín, there was an Intermediate Period of some 1,200 years during which different parts of Peru developed markedly different cultures, in the absence of a horizon culture. This long period was one of prosperity, based on steadily improving agricultural techniques, during which Peruvian farmers learned about irrigation and even fertilizing with guano from sea birds. The population evidently grew, villages expanded into cities, art flourished, and there is ample evidence of successful, established governments. Peru is full of archaeological treasures from these centuries. Of the myriad local cultures, two stand out, in the wealth of their artistic expression and the quantity of material that has survived to the present—thanks large-

ly to the dryness of Peru's coastal deserts. These two cultures are the Moche or Mochica, on the north coast, and the Nazca, on the south.

The Moche civilization emerged in northern Peru in the same valleys that had produced the Chavín and Sechín. It is named after a coastal village that contains the two largest structures built by prehistoric man in South America. These are the gigantic temple mounds known today as the Shrine of the Sun and the Shrine of the Moon. Built entirely of adobe bricks—millions or even billions of them—and added to in successive bursts of construction, they tower above the coastal plain on the scale of the great pyramids of Egypt and Mexico. The larger of the two temple mounds, which shows signs of eight stages of building, contains an occasional grave or evidence of a sacrifice, but the primary purpose of both mounds was to support elevated temples: both are capped by the remains of temples whose plastered walls still show traces of painted frescoes. Similar adobe monuments occur in profusion along the coast of Peru, but none can match those of Moche in vastness.

Moche culture is famous among both archaeologists and collectors for its ceramics. Firm believers in an afterlife, the Moche buried great quantities of fine pottery alongside their dead. These are very beautiful pots, skillfully molded into lifelike figures or shaped into elegant vases and beakers. Most Moche pottery is painted in bright polychrome. Quite apart from the beauty and profusion of this ware, which delight collectors, Moche ceramics have an attribute that has long delighted archaeologists:

From the hands of Moche culture's endlessly inventive potters, a rogues' gallery of striking faces. Left to right: the wizened features of an aged Indian; the startled visage of an aquiline-nosed male whose helmet seems to have come to life; two grim-faced warriors; and the obdurate countenance of a bound captive.

they are vividly realistic, giving us a clear picture of the people who made them. Portrait pots show a wide range of facial types, a gallery that includes sitters with physical deformities, identifiable diseases—even the scars resulting from primitive surgery. Some pots show farming, building, or weaving techniques, and others show fishermen paddling out to sea on reed boats or casting their nets. There are warriors wearing conical helmets and carrying clubs and round shields; there are enemy prisoners, bound and naked; and there are depictions of sacrifice and torture. A frequent subject is runners carrying bags of beans, and some archaeologists have argued that these beans may have carried messages or numerical records, a primitive form of writing. As would be expected from an agricultural society, many pots are shaped like plants, animals, birds, or fish. Others, apparently representations of deities or priests, have human figures with bird or animal faces. Through this pottery alone we have a remarkably complete picture of the dress, customs, and dwellings of the Moche people.

The pottery of Nazca, made on the south coast of Peru at the same time that Moche ware was being created to the north, was very different. It has survived in equal quantities, and it is at once more beautiful and less informative. Nazca potters used shapes broadly similar to those of Moche, but their ceramics were more delicate and the colors more varied and subtle—and Nazca artists never showed scenes of daily life. They sometimes modeled human shapes or painted human figures on vases, but they always confined themselves to priests

or warriors statically posed in full regalia. There are, in addition, some pots in the shape of enemy skulls or trophy heads with the eyes and mouths sewn up, but the Nazcas' favorite and most beautiful subjects were drawn from nature: hummingbirds, leaves, fish, pelicans, and other forms of indigenous flora and fauna, all painted or modeled with great sensitivity in lovely abstract patterns.

The Nazca culture left no monuments to rival the mighty temple platforms, irrigation systems, and defensive walls of the Moche. Instead, they produced an enigmatic legacy that has made the name Nazca famous—the so-called Nazca Lines. The desert around the town of Nazca is marked, over a distance of some 20 miles, with hundreds of mysterious lines. There is no mention of these lines in the Spanish chronicles, and they were virtually unknown until the advent of aviation for it is only by flying over Nazca that one can discern the complicated patterns formed by these enigmatic lines.

The Nazca Lines take many forms. Some are pictorial—a spider monkey, a frigate bird, a killer whale, a spider. Each of these creatures is depicted with great realism, etched onto the desert floor in designs that may measure several hundred yards across. Other designs are abstract—spirals, zigzags, spokes radiating from a hub. In addition there are "plazas," rectangular or trapezoidal stretches of cleared desert, sometimes decorated with lines of stone piles. But the majority of lines are straight, running across the barren countryside for miles on end or crisscrossing one another in bewildering web-like patterns.

No matter what the medium, the Nazca artisans who inhabited southern Peru contemporaneously with the northern Moche preferred stylization to realistic detail. This was true of the potters who produced the jugs seen above and below—the former decorated with a repeating pattern of squids and, below them, trophy heads; the latter, with a single feline figure—and equally true of the anonymous artists who created the gold funerary mask below and the woven cloth pouch shown opposite.

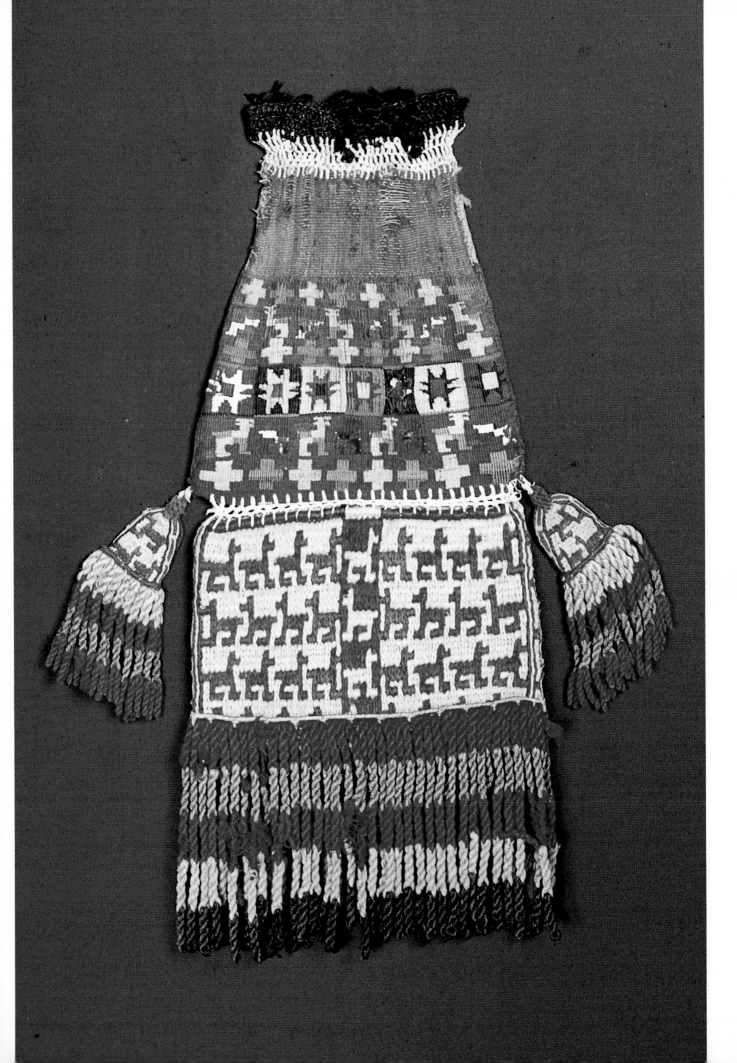

There is no mystery about how the lines were made. The desert near Nazca is covered by a layer of dark, oxydized stones. If this upper layer is pushed aside, the paler sand beneath is exposed. It never rains in this region and there is little wind, so that any disturbance of this stone layer, whether accidental or intentional, will remain visible for centuries. It requires no special skill to scoop these stones aside to form lines a few feet wide, only patience; and it is easy to keep the lines straight by aligning them along three uprights. There is no mystery about who made these lines, either: the designs that depict animals correspond well to those found on Nazca pots. Most pottery found in sites associated with the lines dates from the early phases of Nazca art, the fourth and fifth centuries of the Christian era. The only mystery, then, is *why* the lines were made.

One person who has devoted her life to seeking the answer to the Nazca riddle is Maria Reiche, a German mathematician who has studied the lines for more than thirty years. I first met her in 1960, when she was already the acknowledged authority on the Nazca Lines, living much of the year on the Nazca desert and constantly recording the lines, from the ground, from a stepladder, or bravely strapped to the underside of light aircraft. She is now in her seventies but still working at this puzzle, a tall, thin, handsome lady whose skin is deeply tanned by the desert sun.

Maria Reiche is convinced, after three decades of study, that the Nazca Lines had an astronomical purpose. She points out that ancient Peruvians un-

doubtedly studied and worshiped celestial bodies, particularly along the coastal deserts, where the stars are brilliantly clear. She has recently calculated measurements of the pictorial lines, and from those calculations deduced an ancient unit of measurement based on the human arm—a unit of measure that could have been used to draft the designs. Decades ago, whenever Maria Reiche discovered new lines, she and others cleared away the surface sand to restore the originals. Today, the battle is one of conservation; the lines are world famous, but they are also very vulnerable. Each vehicle driven across this desert creates a new line, and permanently damages the old Nazca patterns. Visitors walking across the fragile surface can also disturb it, as would plans to irrigate and cultivate some of this land. All this must be resisted, and it is largely thanks to the dedication of Maria Reiche that the area of the lines is now protected as an archaeological zone.

Other experts have produced other theories about the Nazca Lines. Paul Kosok, a New York musician turned archaeologist, has argued that some of these drawings were ritual paths. Kosok imagined rows of celebrants moving along the lines; however, the lines are all but invisible from ground level. A much more plausible theory suggests that the Nazcas intended their lines to be seen by deities in heaven. One recent expedition built a hot-air balloon exclusively of materials available to ancient Peruvians, and used this contrivance to soar above the desert. The trouble with this attractive experiment is that something as dramatic as human flight

The German-born mathematician Maria Reiche has devoted the last three decades of her life to an intensive study of the enigmatic Nazca lines, which radiate out for twenty miles in all directions from the ruined remains of that pre-Inca settlement. Created in the fourth and fifth centuries A.D. by brushing away the layer of dark stones that covers the desert surrounding Nazca and revealing the whiter sand beneath, these delicate geometrical traceries are a puzzlement to archaeologists because they can be properly "read" only from the air—from altitudes the Nazca never achieved. Below, Reiche sweeps clean a sinuous Nazca design; at left, she and a young assistant "blue print" a rock painting.

would certainly have been recorded in prehistoric illustration or legend, but it was not.

Dr. Gerald S. Hawkins, a physicist and astronomer formerly with the Smithsonian Institution, also surveyed hundreds of the lines. He then made a list of all astronomical phenomena that occurred over the Nazca desert during the heyday of their culture—the rising and setting of major stars, solstices, eclipses, and the like. He fed all this data into a computer—and reached the sad conclusion that astronomy was not the answer. Although some lines occasionally pointed toward celestial phenomena, this happened so infrequently that it lacked statistical significance. More recently a British investigator, Tony Morrison, has argued that some lines, particularly those that radiate from a nucleus, can be explained as a Nazca equivalent of *ceques*. (Inca *ceque* lines, rows of shrines or holy places, radiate from Cuzco in a manner not unlike the Stations of the Cross along a pilgrimage route.) Morrison also found lines still in use on the Bolivian plateau, where modern Aymara and Quechua Indians have such paths radiating from their villages. Other explanations of the Nazca Lines are less scientific. Some romantics have imagined that they could have been the landing grounds for extraterrestial beings, with one author even resorting to trick photography of the kneecap of the frigate bird design to make this look like a landing pad for flying saucers.

Another famous site that has inspired wild theories is Tiahuanaco. This enormous ruin, just south of Lake Titicaca, stands at 12,000 feet above sea level on the bare Bolivian altiplano. Tiahuanaco is monumental and mysterious enough to have inspired suggestions that it is many thousands of years old, that it antedated the biblical Flood and was later uplifted in some geological cataclysm, and that its vast stone blocks were the work of a race of giants or the landing places for visitors from outer space. The truth, confirmed by extensive excavation and dating, is that the site was occupied throughout the so-called Intermediate Period, during the first millennium of the Christian era, at the same time the Moche and Nazca cultures flourished. By about A.D. 1000, Tiahuanaco had become a vast temple complex, evidently built by thousands of devout laborers. At this time the Tiahuanaco culture extended across almost all of Peru, with the result that there are ruins of the Tiahuanaco civilization in the central and northern Andes. On the coast, the Tiahuanaco style both superseded and obliterated the Nazca and Moche. What is not known is whether this rapid expansion occurred through conquest, trade, or the bursting forth of a new religion. Whatever the reason, Tiahuanaco became the second, or middle, horizon in Peruvian history.

There are four main structures in the Tiahuanaco temple complex. The first is a broad platform called Calasasaya, whose flat surface measures 443 feet by 427 feet and whose sides are retained by sandstone walls of small ashlars alternating with huge upright monoliths. The smaller stones were largely vandalized after the Spanish Conquest. As Bernabé Cobo wrote, "The church of [the Spanish town] of Tiahuanaco was built of these stones, the inhabitants of [La Paz] have taken off a good many

The enigmatic culture that supplanted Moche and Nazca—and the last civilization before the Inca to dominate all of Peru—took its name from its principal temple compound, a sprawling complex at Tiahuanaco near Lake Titicaca. Tiahuanaco culture proved a transient phenomenon, vanishing so completely around A.D. 1200 that the Incas attributed its surviving artifacts, among them the statue seen below, to more ancient peoples.

to construct their houses, and even the Indians of Tiahuanaco make tomb stones of very beautiful dressed stones they take from these ruins." Modern Bolivian archaeologists have restored some of these retaining walls, but with mixed results: the weathered sandstone uprights of the original structure are now interspersed with neatly cemented stones that look more like those we would expect to find in a factory wall than an ancient monument.

To the east of the Calasasaya platform, steps cut into a huge slab of rock lead down to a sunken court measuring some 200 feet square and lined with walls of pink sandstone. The purpose of the rectangular platform and sunken court is unknown, but they are oriented almost exactly to the east and they point toward the place where the sun at its spring solstice rises beside the snow-clad peak of Bolivia's highest mountain, Illimani.

Towering above the Calasasaya platform is an earthen mound called Akapana. The chroniclers Cobo, who visited the ruins in about 1610, and Cieza de León, who was there some sixty years earlier, both recorded that this mound had a stone base. Recent excavations have cleared away the thick cover of earth and grass and exposed this foundation. Akapana is now revealed as a step pyramid, with a base of the finest masonry and a top that may once have been of adobe construction, now weathered into a rounded tumulus.

A few hundred yards to the southwest is the most remarkable of Tiahuanaco's structures, the Puma Punco, or Puma's Gate. It is difficult to reconstruct what was built here, for the ravages of time and

the depredations of treasure-seekers have left a confused jumble of superbly cut stones. There are, for example, the remains of paving cut from immense blocks, from which once rose a series of rectangular doors and windows, all cut with uncanny precision. In some cases the doors, each cut from a single stone, projected from the larger rocks of the flooring platform. As Cieza de León observed:

These huge gateways project from still larger stones on which they were set, some of which were as much as thirty feet wide, fifteen or more long, and six thick: both this and the door, jamb and threshold were one single stone, which was a tremedous phenomenon. When one considers such work, I cannot imagine what kind of machines or tools were used to work them. For it is evident that, before these huge stones were dressed and perfected, they must have been far larger.

A number of enormous statues of gods have been found at Tiahuanaco. These huge stone idols have tall, tubular bodies and stand at attention, their hands holding elaborate scepters. They stare forward from large vacant eyes below which are what archaeologists know as "tear bands"—which add to the baleful, somber majesty of these symbols of a forgotten religion. The most famous Tiahuanaco idol is on the lintel of a large stone gate that stands on top of the Calasasaya platform. The central figure is apparently a sun god, for its head is surrounded by a headdress suggesting the rays of the sun. Rows of forty-eight kneeling, winged

figures, some with human heads and others with condors' beaks, worship the central deity. The gate itself is of hard stone and the carvings are of extraordinary sharpness and precision, so that a mass of complicated detail is still visible after centuries of exposure. Profile heads of condors, pumas, and fish are repeated hundreds of times, as are the sun gods, the scepters, and a distinctive step design. These are the elements of the Tiahuanaco style, and they reappear on pottery, textiles, and stone carvings all over Peru. Such Tiahuanaco decoration is harsh, angular, and forceful—the art of a powerful cult that overwhelmed the more graceful styles of the coastal desert.

Nazca did not survive the impact of Tiahuanaco expansion, but on the north coast of Peru, at a greater geographical distance from Tiahuanaco, a civilization appeared in the twelfth century that was very similar to Moche. This was Chimu, sometimes known as the kingdom of Chimor, which flourished during the four centuries between the sudden expansion of Tiahuanaco and the advent of the more powerful Inca empire. As we noted, Tiahuanaco is known to archaeologists as the middle horizon of Peruvian culture, and the Inca civilization is, of course, the third and last. The three or four centuries between them are therefore known as the Late Intermediate Period, a time when Peruvian culture once again fragmented into tribal states. This was nonetheless a period of prosperity and artistic expression, during which many different cultures thrived in Peru. Chimu was the most luxurious and important of them.

The most consequential of the kingdoms that rose and fell during what is known as the Late Intermediate Period in Peruvian history—the interval between the disappearance of Tiahuanaco and the advent of Inca culture—was the Chimu. In the abundance and luxuriousness of its relics, many of which have survived intact to this day, it reigns supreme over the first centuries of the second millennium A.D., the period when the grim-visaged funerary mask at left and the graceful ceremonial cup below were created by goldsmiths from Chan-chan, the capital of the Chimu empire.

We do not know why the Tiahuanaco epoch was so short-lived. At its height, the Tiahuanaco style took control of an existing empire in the central Andes, and this satellite empire spread outwards from a capital at Huari or Wari (near modern Ayacucho in the mountains midway between Lima and Cuzco). Tiahuanaco-Huari was an urban empire, based on cities and responsible for founding metropolises in many parts of Peru. Its sudden decline may have been the result of tribal resurgence or some form of peasant revolt, for during the Late Intermediate Period, when the Tiahuanaco-Huari civilization did collapse, all the cities of what is now southern Peru and Bolivia declined or disappeared. People reverted to old tribal customs and to life in villages or farming communities, the only exception being the north coast, where the Chimu developed cities that had been founded either in Moche times or during the brief period of the Tiahuanaco horizon.

The most famous city of Chimu was Chan-chan, an immense labryinth of temples, courts, and enclosures that covered almost seven square miles. It was certainly the largest city of prehistoric South America and may have ranked as one of the world's largest cities in its day—as large, for example, as fifteenth-century Paris or Milan. Chan-chan was close to the sea, near the mouth of the Moche River, and since it lay on the dry coastal desert it was inevitably built of adobe bricks, for adobes were by far the most practical and easily attainable building material in that region. The adobe walls of the Chimu capital rested on stone foundations, and

hardwood was used for lintels and roofing beams. Much of the city was built on a massive scale, with city and enclosure walls of great height and thickness built of millions of adobe bricks. The ruin is now desolate and windswept, and the mighty walls have crumbled as a result of centuries of weathering and occasional but very destructive rainfall. In its heyday, Chan-chan was evidently far more attractive. Its walls still show traces of the marvelous arabesque moldings with which they were once adorned. Much of the city was stuccoed and painted with brilliant pictorial and geometric frescoes. The Chimu were also masters of irrigation, and the city was once well watered by a network of channels, pools, and tanks.

Chimu pottery revived many of the themes of its precursor, Moche, but Chimu ceramics are less artistic, colorful, and informative. Chimu potters preferred unpainted black ware, which they created by firing their pottery in closed and smoky ovens, often heightening the black gloss by spreading their pots with metallic glaze. In one respect, Chimu pots *are* informative and even explicit: many of them show sexual activities. Visitors to Lima's Larco Museum can study a room full of "pornographic" Chimu pots that depict people indulging in every known form of sexual activity. The detail on these pots is very graphic, but the activities are shown with engaging frankness and even humor.

Although Chimu pottery was not outstanding, the Chimu did excel in two other art forms: metalworking and textile-making. In both these crafts, the Chimu were merely perfecting techniques that had been developed over many centuries—but they achieved standards of workmanship that are even today unsurpassed anywhere in the world. They mined abundant metals, particularly gold, silver, and copper, and they devised almost all of the possible methods of metalworking known to twentieth-century metallurgists, among them such processes as engraving, lost-wax molding, soldering, gilding, filigree, and, of course, hammering.

Any Chimu objects made of precious metal that still existed at the time of the Conquest were ruthlessly hunted out and melted down by the Spaniards, insatiable in their greed for gold and silver. As a result, any examples of Chimu metalworking now displayed in modern museums have come from recent excavations. Despite this limitation, the quantity and quality are breathtaking. There are lovely pieces of jewelry—necklaces, earrings, arm and leg bands—as well as the more ornate decorations of priests and chiefs—sumptuous headdresses, pectorals, masks, ear discs, and armor. There are also pots and beakers and sculpted figures of people and animals, all crafted with consummate skill.

The quality and variety of Chimu textiles is equally impressive. The Peruvian tradition of excellence in cloth-making went back 1,500 years before the Chimu—to burial shrouds and capes discovered in the dry Paracas peninsula south of Lima and dating from a period shortly after the Chavín horizon. Ancient Peruvian weavers had fine materials to work with, for their llamas, alpaca, and, particularly, the related vicuña produced very fine wool. They also had cotton, one of few plants common to both the Americas and Eurasia in pre-Conquest times. And the Chimu had a fine range of vegetable and mineral dyes, with which they produced colors that have scarcely faded during the intervening centuries. They used tie-dying and embroidery, gauze, lace, and a dazzling repertoire of loom techniques. Weaving was clearly a highly regarded skill in Chimu and earlier societies, where "factories" of male and female artisans worked patiently for years on end to produce textiles of an excellence and beauty unrivaled elsewhere in the world.

Of all the skills of the ancient Peruvians, their textile-making abilities were the most truly outstanding. And with the Chimu, tapestry became a favorite technique and reached the highest possible degree of perfection. The American archaeologist Junius Bird has noted that some Peruvian textiles of the Chimu period achieved 200 or even 250 weft threads per inch, compared with 85 weft threads per inch in early European tapestry and far lower amounts in modern work. "It would be impossible to create such a fabric without having perfect yarn for the warp," Bird observed. "The extreme fineness of weave, however, is only one aspect of the Peruvian product. Every conceivable device applicable to tapestry construction was employed with care and skill." Fortunately, the Spanish conquerors were less interested in cloth than in precious metals, and, the dry climate of the Peruvian coast being an excellent preservative, sufficient early textiles have survived for us to appreciate the skill of Peruvian weavers and marvel at the brilliance of their products.

V

Land of the Four Quarters

The great Inca ruler Pachacuti's victory in A.D. 1438 over the invading Chanca tribe in the hills above Cuzco propelled the Incas into their golden age, a century of unheralded territorial expansion and widening cultural hegemony. During the mid-1400s, as we have noted, Inca armies occupied the Vilcabamba hills immediately north of their homeland. Then, striking alternately north and south, they conquered the Chanca, Colla, and Lupaca lands near Lake Titicaca and the region around Tiahuanaco. Pachacuti's son Tupac Inca Yupanqui proved to be as formidable a military leader as his father, and it was he who pushed the empire's frontiers northward along the line of the Andes. Centuries of acclimatization to high altitudes had given the Incas the enlarged lungs and spleens and the high red corpuscle counts associated with mountain peoples, enabling them to breathe the thin air of the high Andes—and it was therefore natural that their first conquests should be in the mountains. In ensuing decades, tribe after tribe was absorbed into the growing empire.

Once the mountain valleys and passes were secure, the Incas were ready to descend to the dry coastal plains along the Pacific coast. They simply outflanked the rich kingdom of Chimu, which lay on the Peruvian littoral, and then swept down from the hills to defeat it. Chan-chan and the other great cities of the northern coast fell to the Incas; Tupac Inca then turned his attention south, taking the Rimac valley around modern Lima and the holy shrine of Pachacamac a few miles south of that city. Advancing southward, Inca armies conquered valley after valley, sometimes after prolonged fighting but more often after peaceful submission. By 1490 they had taken the entire south coast of Peru, the area in which Nazca culture had once flourished. Other campaigns pushed Inca rule across the Bolivian altiplano and into the valleys of central Chile.

By the time of Tupac Inca's death in 1493—a mere fifty-five years after Pachacuti's victory over the Chanca—the Inca empire stretched some 2,500 miles, from southern Chile to beyond Quito in what is now northern Ecuador. In little more than half a century the Incas had established the third, or late, horizon of Peruvian archaeology, an empire far surpassing those of Chavín or Tiahuanaco.

We know much about the Incas' methods of winning and controlling their vast territory—from the chronicles of the conquistadores, from interrogations of aged Indians that the Spaniards conducted soon after the Conquest, and from recent archaeological excavations. The Incas resorted to warfare only when peaceful coercion failed, and as Bernabé Cobo suggested, coercion succeeded with increasing frequency as Inca might grew: "Reports of the extraordinary victories and of the power of the Inca reached the most distant lands and struck terror into their chief and rulers. These would send envoys to offer submission, begging to be accepted as his vassals. He graciously and cordially welcomed those who submitted voluntarily, but he savagely attacked those who resisted."

There was nothing revolutionary about Inca fighting methods. Soldiers wore short tunics, not unlike those worn by imperial Roman troops, and they

Two aryballi and a jug (left) from the burial caves at Machu Picchu.

went into battle bare-legged and either barefoot or wearing simple sandals. Their only armor was a wooden or metal-plated helmet, a wood and cloth shield, and round metal discs fastened on their chests and backs. They used such traditional weapons as clubs and battle-axes, some with sharp stone blades, others with star- or donut-shaped stone or bronze heads. The soldiers also favored the slingshot, and every Inca warrior wore a headband that unwound to form a sling. Some soldiers used spear-throwers to hurl javelins, but there was little use of bows and arrows, presumably because suitable woods for them were scarce in the Andes. Inca generals did sometimes enlist warriors from primitive jungle tribes, however, and these were usually brilliant archers.

Although adept at cunning stratagems to penetrate enemy defenses, the Incas' basic battle tactics involved simple maneuvers by phalanxes of club-wielding warriors. Their fighting methods may have been primitive, but there was nothing backward about their communications or logistics. Much of their success in battle was a direct result of the construction, as the empire expanded, of a splendid network of roads, provincial garrisons, and storage depots. Having no draft animals or wheeled vehicles, the Incas built their roads exclusively for walking men and trains of llamas. These roads were often stepped, climbing successive mountain ranges.

The Incas needed all of their considerable engineering skills to drive pathways through the vertiginous world of the Andes. At times the roads ran through tunnels carved from living rock, and

only on the coastal desert did they resemble conventional highways—wide, and lined with earth dikes. Just as important as these roads were the bridges that spanned the innumerable canyons, ravines, torrents, and rivers of the Incas' mountainous empire. Small streams were bridged by stone slabs corbeled out from the riverbanks; broad, flat rivers were spanned by pontoons of reed or balsawood floats. But for rivers in deep mountain canyons, the Incas created suspension bridges. At the very point where the rivers were narrowest and most terrifying—and their waters most constricted—Inca engineers erected great stone foundations on either bank. Thick wooden beams were laid across this stonework, and thick osier cables made fast to them and stretched across the river. When half a dozen of these cables had been joined, they were interwoven with strong hemp and reinforced with sticks. This done, the walkway was edged on either side. It hung suspended in midair, far above the water.

The first conquistadores were apprehensive about these swaying contraptions, which they feared their horses would refuse to cross. It seemed impossible to imagine horses—animals that weigh so much and are so timorous and excitable—crossing something suspended in the air. But although the beasts refused at first, once they were driven onto a bridge they crossed calmly, one behind the other.

Having built their fine network of roads, the Incas ensured that traffic moved rapidly along them: Post runners called *chasqui* were stationed at regular intervals on the royal highways, and each town or village had to keep a complement of men ready

to race along these roads with messages or packets for the Inca and his nobles. It was claimed that the royal court in Cuzco received fresh fish daily from the Pacific Ocean, carried by relays of runners for hundreds of miles over two ranges of mountains. In fact, messages moved across Peru faster in the days of the Incas than at any subsequent time until the invention of the modern telegraph. When the Inca himself or any of his high officials moved through the empire, they traveled in litters borne by runners from a tribe that was famous for its agility. Along the route, they stayed in posthouses called *tambos,* constructed at regular intervals.

There was also a network of provincial capital cities, spaced a few days' march apart along the royal highways. Although many of these towns were newly built by the Incas, they were unwalled and had surprisingly little in the way of formal fortifications, the Incas choosing to rely instead on the speed of their communications, the excellence of their roads, and the prowess of their armies to control their enormous territory.

The Incas called their empire Tawantin-suyu, the Land of the Four Quarters. Cuzco was the center of the world. To the east, toward the rising sun, lay the Anti-suyu, a land of Amazonian forests and jungle tribes only loosely dominated by the highland Incas. To the west, between Cuzco and the ocean, was the Cunti-suyu, from the word for the setting sun. To the south was the far larger Colla-suyu, named after the Colla tribe near Lake Titicaca but stretching for hundreds of miles into Chile.

And to the north lay the largest and most prosperous *suyu,* or quarter, the Chincha-suyu, also named after an important tribe.

Each quarter was governed by a prefect or army commander. These high officials were of royal blood and formed a council of state to advise the emperor in Cuzco. Their *suyus* were divided into many provinces, most of which corresponded to geographical or tribal areas, and these provinces were in turn administered by powerful governors. Below these was an administrative pyramid, with ranks of officials arranged according to a decimal system: chiefs governing 10,000 tribute-payers, then those supervising 1,000, 100, and so on down to only 10 tribute-payers.

The Inca state was totalitarian, with every aspect of the subjects' lives controlled by the imperial administration. The entire lifetimes of both men and women were divided into discrete age groups, with specific tasks allotted to each. Children, for instance, were put to tending flocks of llamas, while adolescents performed agricultural tasks or felled wild birds with their slings. State officials even went around the villages arranging marriages between young men and women of appropriate age, at the same time selecting girls for service as *mamaconas,* or chosen women, assessing quotas of tribute produce, and assigning military or labor service to be performed by adult men. There was also complete control of movement, language, and even the dress of the empire's citizens. The Inca system managed to combine an absolute hereditary monarchy with

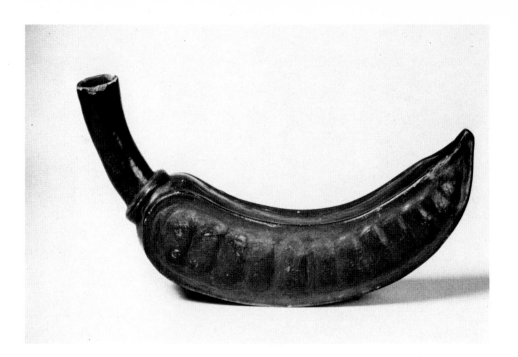

a communistic welfare state, and despite all the controls it seems to have worked rather well. Under Inca rule peasants were freed from intertribal wars and benefited from being part of an empire that sought to keep them well-fed and contented.

The secret of Inca success was that the empire managed to produce not only ample goods and foodstuffs for its armies, religious officials, and the luxurious court at Cuzco but plenty for the common people. The Inca himself granted local chieftains permission to distribute cloth and food from the state stores to needy peasants—a practice that kept their subjects contented. Surplus goods were often taken from one province to another, some finding their way from the plains to the mountains and vice versa, depending on where the shortfall occurred in a given season.

The forethought and efficiency of Inca administration may sound utopian, but the Spanish invaders saw ample proof of the effectiveness of this national policy of storage and redistribution when they marched into Peru. Along their invasion route they found hundreds of storage huts, called *qollqas* by the Incas, at every provincial center, and they discovered that the Incas had even perfected methods of dehydrating food for storage. The native Indian chronicler Felipe Huaman Poma wrote that in the region around Lake Titicaca the people stored frozen, dried potatoes; cooked, dried potatoes; cooked, frozen sorrel tuber; and dried meat. In all parts of the kingdom they stockpiled maize, sweet potatoes, chili peppers, coca, and various other foods that could be eaten without prior cooking.

The *qollqa* generally stood just outside populated areas, in high, cool, airy locations near the royal roads. A typical storage depot consisted of many square buildings as small as ordinary rooms, set in tidy lines like little towers and spaced two or three yards apart. The high locations were chosen to protect the contents from damp, and the spacing of the huts was protection against fire.

Pedro de Cieza de León saw hundreds of these storehouses, all filled with provisions, when he toured the Inca empire in the 1540s. At Tumibamba (modern Cuenca, in what is now Ecuador), the royal stores were so comprehensive that "when the Lord Inca was lodged in his palace and his soldiers garrisoned there, nothing, from the most important to the most trivial item, could not be provided." At Vilcashuamán, another important Inca city, the Spanish chronicler noted 700 *qollqas*. His observations are confirmed by modern archaeology. A site in eastern Bolivia contains the ruins of no less than 2,400 huts, all 10 feet square and arranged in rows, each precisely 17 feet from its neighbors. During recent excavations at the provincial Inca city of Huánuco in central Peru, the American archaeologist Craig Morris studied the remains of 497 storage huts and found that their design differed slightly for the storage of different types of products.

These provincial storehouses were unquestionably impressive, but those of the capital city were truly remarkable. Pedro Sancho, for one, marveled over Cuzco's *qollqas* for goods grown or manufactured in the country: "There are shields, leather bucklers, beams for roofing houses, knives and oth-

According to Bernabé Cobo, who left one of the most detailed records of the invasion of Peru, the Incas' system of food redistribution was a marvel of efficiency: "There was no lack in any area and none suffered want even in meager years. They distributed enough rations for everyday requirements, but whatever was left over was kept in storehouses for time of need." In addition to grain, Cobo observed, these qollqa, *or storehouses, contained jerked llama meat, cotton and wool for weaving, and weapons used to provision troops. The influence of Indian agriculture on Indian art is evident in the ceramic whistle at left, shaped like a seed pod, and the jug at right, whose body is composed of ripe ears of corn.*

er tools, sandals and breastplates to equip the soldiers. All was in such vast quantities that it is hard to imagine how the natives can ever have paid such immense tribute of so many items."

Such huge stocks of produce required careful bookkeeping, and although the Incas did not have writing they did invent a mnemonic device for recording numbers. This was the *quipu,* an arrangement of strings hanging like a tassle from a master cord. Each string was knotted at various points along its length with knots of different size, which sometimes incorporated different-colored threads. The secret of reading *quipus* is lost forever, but it seems clear that each strand had a meaning to the sender and recipient, and that the number of loops in each knot indicated quantity.

Inca taxation consisted of labor levies as well as produce; each agricultural community, in addition to laboring in its fields, was obliged to provide men and women for all forms of imperial service. Some years after the Conquest Peru's Spanish overlords interrogated the oldest of their Inca subjects about the tribute they had provided in the days of the empire. One of these formal inquiries has survived, a deposition taken in a district alongside Lake Titicaca that provides impressive insights into the working of the Inca state. In it, an old chief recalls that his tribe had sent the Inca many men, some to serve in the army and others to build his palaces in Cuzco. Both male and female Indians served in the royal household, and daughters of chiefs became the Inca's handmaidens. The old chief's tribe also sent to Cuzco men and women who were sacrificed to the idols in the shrines, and Indians who were resettled as colonists in conquered lands. They also provided the labor that built agricultural terraces and gave the ruler fine cloth and llamas for tribute. Conscripts also mined gold at La Paz and silver at Porco, and those who did not serve lavished their spiritual and temporal leader with gifts: featherwork, sandals, jerked meat, and wool from communally owned llamas; *llautus,* or head ornaments; and slings for battle, copper battle-axes, and copper clamps for the stone blocks of the royal buildings.

The conscript levies moved readily about the empire, thanks to the splendid Inca roads—which had, of course, been built by similar levies—and they consumed food from the state stores along their route. When they reached one of the provincial capitals, they were lodged in vast *kallankas,* halls similar to those attached to the palaces in Cuzco, which had been constructed specifically for this purpose. One young Spanish priest observed that some *kallankas* were more than 150 yards long and very broad and spacious. Large numbers of people could be housed in each of these well-roofed, well-appointed, and clean halls, whose many doors admitted plenty of light. Each overnight visitor was provided with a daily ration, and each took his food in turn, "without any bustle, just as if they had been monks—for the common people of this land were the most obedient, humble and disciplined that I believe could be found anywhere on earth."

The young priest was correct to stress the docility of Andean Indians, for that may have been the sa-

Peru is a hostile land, its extremes of climate and altitude a challenge to all who chose to make their home there. It is small wonder, then, that the Incas, who mastered the heights and the harsh weather of the Andes, found themselves equal to the hostility of the conquistadores. With resilience to match their notable docility, the Indians of the Peruvian altiplano deferred to their conquerors without surrendering their cultural heritage to them. As a result, today's descendants of the Incas bear a striking resemblance to their ancestors, not only in physiognomy but in clothing, in custom, and in their attitude toward foreigners.

lient quality of their national make-up. Indeed, their descendants are just as obedient as their forebears reportedly were: they seem almost cowed, but possessed of a tenacious resilience that can endure almost any amount of hardship, privation, or hunger. This humility and discipline made the peasants perfect subjects for the Incas' benevolent despotism. Ironically, this same deference to authority was a crucial weakness when the empire was threatened by invasion. As long as the Indians were led into battle by Inca officers, they fought well; but, deprived of leadership, they showed themselves to be without initiative or individual will, and they readily capitulated to the Spanish conquerors.

Another weakness of the Inca empire was the fact that it was an amalgam of recently subdued tribal states. As we have noted, the Incas conquered their vast domain in less than a half-century. In so doing they seem to have discovered most of the techniques of successful imperialism. They preferred peaceful persuasion to force of arms, for instance, and they honored the chiefs of those tribes that surrendered easily, by allowing them a panoply of authority even though real power lay with centrally appointed Inca officials. The sons of subdued chieftains were brought to the court of Cuzco for education and indoctrination in Inca ways, and the idols revered by conquered peoples were taken to Cuzco to be worshiped alongside Inca deities. In truth, of course, these minor princes and tribal totems were hostages, ensuring the good behavior of their peoples.

By the beginning of the sixteenth century the Incas had adopted another classic colonialist device—the establishment of communities of loyal colonists, known as *mitmaes,* in conquered regions. This tactic, together with the hostage system and the mobility of the Inca armies, kept the empire reasonably peaceful. Occasional revolts by subject tribes were ruthlessly suppressed, as when Tupac Inca was obliged to hurry south from his campaign in central Peru to put down a rising of the rich tribes around Lake Titicaca.

The ever-restive Cañari of southern Ecuador were conquered by Tupac Inca's successor, Huayna Capac. They rebelled against his son Atahualpa, however, and the men of the tribe were promptly slaughtered in a battle at Yaguar-cocha, the Lake of Blood. Rather than risk such fury, most tribes happily accepted the benefits of Inca civilization, which kept its subjects well fed, cushioned against famine in bad years, free from intertribal wars, entertained by a steady round of official celebrations, and living in regimented rural tranquillity.

Most Andean Indians accepted their ordered society, a world of village communities offering little latitude for individual expression or ambition. The state demanded absolute conformity, as do tribes of forest Indians in Amazonia to this day; in exchange, it provided absolute security. So absolute, in fact, that the conquistadores marveled at the fact that the inhabitants had no locks on their houses. Before departing, one simply placed a stick over the entrance, confident that no possessions would be touched. Any individual who did break established laws and customs was despised by society

and punished by the state, and the chronicles describe a scale of harsh punishments for crimes ranging from adultery, abuse of royal possessions, sorcery, and common theft to murder and treason. For the most serious offenses, the penalty was death, either by stoning, clubbing, or being thrown from a high precipice. And, for habitual criminals, execution was by "hanging upside down and left hanging in this way until they died."

There was a prison in Cuzco, in the district below the sun temple Coricancha, known as the Puma's Tail. According to the chronicler Huaman Poma, it was "constructed below ground in the form of a crypt, very dark, in which they raised snakes, poisonous serpents, pumas, jaguars, bears, foxes, dogs, wildcats, vultures, and eagles—creatures that could be used to punish criminals and delinquents." Hiram Bingham identified one sector of Machu Picchu as a prison: a walled, triangular enclosure below the main squares that divide the city. One side was bounded by a magnificent three-storied house with sweeping views of the Urubamba valley—and Bingham thought that this might have been the residence of the judge or prison governor. The enclosure contained subterranean passages similar to Huaman Poma's crypt full of deadly beasts; and an outcropping of rock on the floor of this crypt had been shaped to resemble the head and beak of the world's largest bird of prey—the condor. In an upper gallery were a row of full-length niches with holes bored through their stone sides. These could have been the scene of the upside-down hangings described in the chronicles.

A less frightening symbol of Inca rule was the ceremonial platform that stood in the center of the broad royal square at the heart of every provincial city. A high stairway led up to the rectangular platform. The Inca and three retainers would ascend to address the people and to review their troops. This reviewing platform was called an *usnu,* which the Inca dictionary defined as a judge's tribunal.

In a society where the state and its official religion were so closely interrelated, *usnus* were bound to have religious as well as administrative functions, and we know from the chronicles that on such platforms sacrifices were offered to the sun in its different phases, with *chicha,* or maize beer, poured out in its honor. One chronicler wrote of the Inca going "to pray on an elegant and excellent terrace that had been built for that purpose. They sacrificed . . . the things that they usually sacrificed, killing many animals and birds." A number of these "elegant and excellent" terraces survive in ruined Inca cities. The largest of all is at Huánuco, in the mountains north of Lima. It is a building that in many ways epitomizes Inca architecture—massive, built of painstakingly perfect masonry, and devoid of decoration in the characteristically austere Inca manner. Huánuco's *usnu* is long and squat: its top covers an area of roughly 100 feet by 165 feet, but the platform rises only 13 feet above its base. It has a core of solid earth and is faced on all sides with fine Inca masonry; the top is enclosed by a parapet and approached by a broad flight of steps. It stands in the midst of a gigantic plaza, the size of two football fields, a fitting symbol of Inca authority.

By the 1520s Tawantin-suyu, the Inca Land of the Four Quarters, occupied most of the Pacific coast of South America. The Incas were in full control of modern Ecuador, and Inca armies were fighting far to the north in what is now southern Colombia, attempting to occupy the provinces of Pasto and Popayán. Had they succeeded, they would have reached near the headwaters of the Cauca and Magdalena rivers, and they might have pushed on to overcome the gold-rich tribes of Colombia, thereby extending their empire to the Caribbean.

The Inca Huayna Capac, Pachacuti's grandson, loved the northern part of his empire. The Andes of Ecuador enclose delightful valleys that are lower and more fertile than the traditional Inca homeland around Cuzco, and Huayna Capac built the great cities of Quito and Tumibamba (modern Cuenca) in this northern region. It was said that he contemplated dividing the empire and creating a second capital in one of these cities, making it the Cuzco of the north.

After he had completed his campaigns in what is now southern Colombia and secured the northern reaches of his empire, the Inca Huayna Capac returned to Tumibamba, residing in this northern city for ten years and seemingly content to settle permanently in its perfect climate. It was during Huayna Capac's years at Tumibamba, however, that the calm of the Inca empire was shattered by a strange phenomenon. In the spring of 1528 word reached the royal palace that a strange people, never before seen in those parts, had arrived in ships off the coast of the empire and were asking what

land they had reached. These strangers, as unexpected and unfamiliar as visitors from another planet, were of course the first Spaniards.

Some time after the appearance of the first Spanish ship, another ominous event occurred—a terrible epidemic in which countless people died from a disease described as a combination of measles and incurable leprosy. Huayna Capac himself died of it, and his subjects embalmed him and took him to Cuzco for burial. One chronicler, who described the epidemic as a great pestilence of smallpox, noted that it was so contagious that some 200,000 people died of it in all districts. The Incas lost not only their beloved ruler but also his eldest son and heir and a large part of the court and senior government officials. The deadly disease almost certainly *was* smallpox, for it is known that this disease crossed the Atlantic at about this time, carried by infected sailors in a Spanish ship. Its impact on the New World was utterly devastating: native Americans had no defenses against this hitherto unknown disease, and they died then in the thousands. It is difficult to exaggerate the importance of smallpox and other "imported" diseases in demoralizing and destroying the native populations of the Americas and opening their lands to European invasion. In all probability the disease introduced by the conquistadores spread from tribe to tribe across modern Colombia, from the shores of the Caribbean to the northern part of the Inca empire—where, by decimating the Incas' ruling hierarchy, it left Tawantin-suyu leaderless, racked by internecine struggles, and vulnerable to attack.

VI

Sweat of the Sun, Tears of the Moon

In 1478, fourteen years before Christopher Columbus discovered the New World, two men were born in western Spain who were to play important roles in the European exploration of the Pacific. One was Francisco Pizarro, illegitimate son of an army officer and a servant; the other was Vasco Núñez de Balboa, a well-born but impoverished adventurer. Balboa first saw the Americas while serving as a page on an exploratory voyage, and he later stowed away with his dog on a fleet bound for Panama's Caribbean coast. Before long Balboa had become mayor of a tiny outpost on the Darien coast—the first formal Spanish settlement on the American mainland.

A local chieftain soon told the new mayor of a province to the south that was rich in the very gold the Spaniards sought with such fervor. The Indian informant also spoke of another sea, where people traveled in ships with sails and oars. This inspired Balboa to plunge inland, climbing native paths through forests drenched by the highest annual rainfall in all the Americas. On September 25, 1513, his perseverance was rewarded: his expedition, having crossed the narrow Isthmus of Panama, gazed down on the blue waters of the Pacific. It took the party four more days to descend to the Pacific shore, where Balboa waded into the waters to claim for Spain an ocean that he named the South Sea. By 1519 the Spaniards had founded a settlement called Panama on that shore.

Rumors of rich lands to the south continued to reach the Spaniards who settled in Panama—one report identified the ruler of this wealthy people as Birú or Peru—and a number of expeditions began to investigate the bleak Pacific shores of what is now Colombia. Then, in 1524, command of a ship that had been built on the new ocean passed to Francisco Pizarro, who was by then a relatively prosperous citizen of Panama, a veteran of many expeditions along its Caribbean shores, and, by contemporary standards, aged. He was in his forties.

Pizarro managed to obtain a royal license to discover and conquer the unknown land, but his early voyages were disastrous failures. There were landings on the inhospitable Pacific coast of South America, skirmishes with primitive but fierce tribes, and periods of near starvation. It was only at the beginning of 1527, when his ship at last sailed south of the equator, that Pizarro's men finally caught a glimpse of the rich land of Birú/Peru. They captured an ocean-going Inca sailing raft bound on a trading voyage up the coast of modern Ecuador, and a breathless report on this thrilling discovery was sent to Spain. Gold objects, in combination with the magnificent textiles found on board the raft, were the first sign of an advanced civilization that Pizarro's men had encountered.

Pizarro was in no position immediately to follow up this first contact with the Incas, for his men were dying of disease and privation. They were obliged to winter on a deserted island off the shore of southern Colombia, where some of the more mutinous managed to smuggle out an appeal for help on a ship that was returning to Panama. This resulted in the arrival of two ships, dispatched by the governor of Panama, with an authorization per-

Inca jewelry unearthed at Machu Picchu includes this necklace made of small copper disks.

mitting any man who wished to do so to abandon the seemingly hopeless enterprise. Whereupon Pizarro issued what was to become a legendary challenge. He drew a line in the sand with his sword point and invited all brave men to follow him across it for further adventure, saying: "On that side you go to Panama, to remain poor; on this side, to Peru to be rich. Any of you who would be good Spaniards, choose which you prefer." Thirteen men accepted the challenge and crossed the line.

After six more months of solitude, hunger, and suffering—particularly from mosquitoes—Pizarro and his handful of followers were visited by a ship captained by the noted navigator Bartolomé Ruiz. Pizarro, still obsessed by his vision of great wealth, persuaded Ruiz to join him in a voyage of discovery to the south. This was purely an exploratory journey, for the ship had none of the horses, men, or weapons needed for an invasion. Ruiz and Pizarro soon sighted more ocean-going rafts, however, and they followed the fragile fleet to their home port, Tumbes in northern Peru. From Tumbes the explorers sailed south along the coast of Peru, sighting more towns and becoming increasingly aware of both the size and power of this strange empire. There is little question that it was this landing at Tumbes that was reported to Huayna Capac in Tumibamba.

Pizarro now suspected that a civilization as rich and as memorable as that of the Aztecs of Mexico, conquered by the Spaniards under Hernán Cortés in 1519, awaited subjugation in Peru. He therefore returned to Spain to recruit men, raise money, and

obtain, from the king himself, the title of governor of the land he planned to seize. By January 1531 Pizarro was back in Panama and set sail with an expeditionary force of 180 men and 37 horses. Ignorant of the geography of the Pacific coast, Pizarro landed his men on the shores of what is now Ecuador. This mistake cost the expedition a full year, during which they struggled down the difficult, heavily forested coast. There were occasional battles with warriors from coastal tribes, and it was not until Easter 1532 that the invaders finally reached the northern tip of the Inca empire.

The empire in 1532 was measurably weaker than it had been in the days of Huayna Capac Inca a few years earlier. When Huayna Capac and his immediate heir died in the smallpox epidemic that struck his court, the succession was disputed by two of the ruler's younger sons. This was not the first time there had been a dispute over the succession, but in this instance it led to a bitter civil war that left the empire sadly vulnerable to the menace of European invasion. The contenders for the Inca title were Huascar, the more legitimate successor, who resided at Cuzco and had the support of the royal establishment; and Atahualpa, a son of Huayna Capac by a subsidiary wife. He made his headquarters at Quito and had the support of the army and the northern provinces. After a series of battles fought along the length of the Andes, Atahualpa's faction emerged victorious. The veteran generals Chalcuchima, Quisquis, and Rumiñavi swept south and occupied all the important towns between Quito and Cuzco. And—just as Pizarro's

tiny force was entering Peru—Quisquis won a final victory outside Cuzco and captured Huascar and his entourage in the capital. When this good news reached Atahualpa, he began to march south.

Pizarro's small band, making its way down the northern coast of Peru, also learned of Quisquis' victory and thus became aware, for the first time, of the bitterness of Peru's internecine quarrel. The town of Tumbes, which had been so prosperous four years previously, was now in ruins, filled with the executed victims of this imperial strife. Pizarro knew how successfully Cortés had manipulated rival factions during his conquest of Mexico, and he naturally hoped to repeat such tactics.

He spent the next months advancing slowly across Peru's northern coastal desert, pausing to found a Spanish port near modern Piura. His men were heartened by the arrival of reinforcements in two more ships, one of them led by the dashing Hernando de Soto. Not until September 1532 did Pizarro finally embark on his bid to penetrate—and, conceivably, to overthrow—the mighty Inca empire. He had a total of 168 men at his command, of whom 62 were mounted and the rest marched on foot. Their leader was now in his fifties, thin, weatherbeaten, and fanatically determined. Unable to ride well and illiterate into the bargain, Pizarro was more Don Quixote than dashing conqueror—seemingly no threat whatsoever to the mighty Incas. An Inca official who visited Pizarro's camp at this time carefully observed the Europeans' swords and horses and concluded that these strangers were too bedraggled and disorganized to be a serious menace.

As they marched, the invading Spaniards began to observe the wonders of Inca organization. At one point, Pizarro sent de Soto on a week-long reconnaissance into the mountains, and when the latter reached the provincial town of Caxas he encountered an *aclla-huasi* full of chosen women. In the words of de Soto's companion Diego de Trujillo, "there were in that town three houses of cloistered women called *mamaconas*. When we entered, the women were brought out into the square—over five hundred of them—and the Captain [de Soto] gave many of them to the Spaniards. An Inca official grew very angry and said: 'How dare you do this, when Atahualpa is only twenty leagues from here! Not a man among you will remain alive!' "

So the victorious Atahualpa was in the mountains, and not far from the Spaniards' line of march. This was an opportunity too good to pass up, and on November 8, 1532, Pizarro led his men boldly up into the Andes to meet the Inca. Their advance was continuously monitored by Inca sentries, but there was no opposition. A week later the Spaniards descended into the fertile mountain valley of Cajamarca, where Atahualpa was camped with an army of some 30,000 men. On the very evening that the Spaniards reached Cajamarca, an embassy was sent to the Inca, who was relaxing in the natural hot baths that bubbled from the ground a few miles from the town. As these horsemen advanced to meet the emperor, they passed through the midst of the Inca army. The small party moved with trepidation past the silent ranks of the Inca soldiers and eventually reached the presence of Atahualpa.

"*Atahualpa came in a very fine litter with the ends of its timbers covered in silver,*" *wrote an awed eyewitness to the first encounter between the Inca monarch and the small force led by Francisco Pizarro. "His own person was most richly dressed, with a crown on his head and a collar of large emeralds around his neck," the chronicler noted, adding that Atahualpa's litter was "lined with parrot feathers of many colors and embellished with plates of gold and silver." Below: a sixteenth-century portrait of the Inca ruler—without emeralds. At left: a silver basin commemorating the Conquest. Pizarro, bearded, and Atahualpa, in characteristic headgear, appear at center.*

Atahualpa was wearing the royal insignia, a tassel that fell from the front of the sling-cord that every Indian wore around his head. In the Inca's case, the royal *llautu,* or head ornament, was of very fine scarlet wool, cut very evenly and cleverly held toward the middle by small gold bugles. The inch-thick tassel fell to his eyebrows and covered his entire forehead. The Inca greeted the foreigners with great dignity, making no movement even when the breath from de Soto's horse stirred the royal fringe. There was a conversation, translated by an interpreter, a boy captured four years previously on the ocean-going raft and subsequently taught Spanish by his captors.

Horses had existed in South America in prehistoric times, long before the Ice Age and the arrival of the first humans. But by the early Christian era they were extinct, and the animals brought by the conquistadores were entirely new to the Peruvians. During this first large-scale encounter between the Spanish and the Indians, Atahualpa examined these alien creatures closely. Noting the Inca's interest, Hernando de Soto called for a small horse that had been trained to rear up, and asked the Inca whether he wanted him to ride it in the courtyard. Atahualpa indicated that he did, and de Soto led the beast around the enclosure. "The nag was spirited," one observer recalled, "and made much foam at its mouth. [Atahualpa] was amazed by this and at the agility with which it wheeled."

As a result of this initial meeting the Inca invited the foreigners to lodge in Cajamarca, promising to come in person the following day to meet their

Gaining by deceit what they could not have secured through direct assault, the Spanish invaders of the Inca empire turned the occasion of their second audience with Atahualpa into a surreptitious attack upon the unsuspecting and unarmed Inca ruler (seen at center in the fanciful eighteenth-century Flemish engraving at left). When the dust finally cleared on the plains outside Cajamarca, Atahualpa was in chains, many of his lieutenants were dead or dying, and the Inca army was in flight. After congratulating Pizarro on his victory one conquistador confessed in his diary: "That day, six or seven thousand Indians lay dead on the plain and many more had their arms cut off or other wounds."

leader. The Spaniards were in a quandary: "All were full of fear, for we were so few and were so deep in the land where we could not be reinforced," wrote one. "All assembled in [Pizarro's] quarters to debate what should be done the following day. . . . Few slept and we kept watch in the square, from which the camp fires of the Indian army could be seen. It was a fearful sight. The Spaniards resolved to prepare an ambush, to attempt nothing less than the seizure of the Inca himself. Francisco Pizarro was to decide at the last moment whether to put this audacious plan into action.

The main square of Cajamarca was ideally suited to the Spaniards' purpose, for long, low buildings lined three sides of the square, and men could be concealed in these. Each building had some twenty doors letting onto the square, and if Pizarro were to order the surprise attack, all were to charge out of these structures, the horsemen already mounted. Other soldiers were posted to block the few streets that entered the square. In its center was the customary *usnu*, or platform, which was approached by a stone staircase. Pizarro stationed his Greek gunner Pedro de Candia on the *usnu* and entrusted him with the expedition's small cannon—to be fired at a prearranged signal from the commander.

The following day was Saturday, November 16, 1532. The Spaniards waited anxiously in their hiding places for hours, but the Inca failed to appear. They were in an impasse: If they did nothing, it was likely they would be killed as punishment for the outrages they had committed since reaching Peru; if they attacked and failed, however, death

was certain. They had seen Atahualpa's large and disciplined army, but they had no experience of how bravely or how well these Indians fought. Finally, in the late afternoon, news came that the Inca was approaching in a magnificent litter, accompanied by thousands of his men. It is hardly surprising that the young page Pedro Pizarro recorded having seen some of his companions urinate out of pure terror, seemingly without noticing it.

Atahualpa's arrival could hardly have been more impressive. As he approached, the entire plain filled with men who rearranged their parade formations at every step. All the Indians wore ceremonial clothes and had large gold and silver discs on their heads. In front was a squadron wearing colorful livery that was checkered like a chessboard, and as they advanced they removed straws from the ground and swept the roadway. They swung their arms to the ground in unison, chanting a song as they did so. As the sun was sinking, the Inca himself entered the square with about 6,000 unarmed men. Behind came the litters and hammocks of other important lords. Squadrons of attendants clad in gold and silver headdresses entered the square, and as each group arrived it parted to make way for others behind.

Atahualpa was surprised to see no Spaniards in the square, and he called out to them, thinking they had hidden from fear. At this, a Dominican friar named Vicente de Valverde advanced toward the Inca's litter with the boy interpreter. Atahualpa demanded the return of everything seized or consumed by the Spaniards since their arrival in his realm. Valverde began delivering the Requirement, an extraordinary document that the Spanish royal council had decreed must be proclaimed in any conquest before troops resorted to bloodshed. The friar explained that the holy doctrine to which he referred was contained in the breviary he was holding, and Atahualpa ordered him to surrender the book. The Inca had trouble opening it, however, so the friar extended an arm to assist him—only to be struck on the arm with great disdain. The Inca had never seen writing, let alone a book, and he clearly found it incomprehensible when he did succeed in getting it open. He leafed through it, admiring its form and layout, but after examining it he angrily threw it down among his men, his face turning a deep crimson. The interpreter ran to fetch it and handed it to Valverde.

The critical moment had come. Atahualpa stood up in his litter and called on his men. Valverde returned to the other Spaniards, weeping and shouting: "Come out! Come out, Christians! Come at these enemy dogs who reject the things of God. That chief has thrown my book of holy law to the ground! March out against him, for I absolve you!" Pizarro made his decision: he gave the agreed signal, and the gunner on the *usnu* fired his cannon. Spaniards in full armor charged their horses straight into the packed mass of unarmed natives. "They had all placed rattles on their horses to terrify the Indians," an eyewitness related. "With the booming of the shots, and the trumpets, and the troop of horses with their rattles, the Indians were thrown into confusion and panicked. The Spaniards fell upon them and began to kill." Panic-stricken Incas trampled and crushed one another, trying to escape the murderous charge, but the Spanish horsemen rode right over them, pressing home the attack. The unarmed Indians were routed.

Pizarro, who had stationed himself with a contingent of foot-soldiers, now advanced directly toward Atahualpa's litter. He fearlessly grabbed the Inca's left arm and shouted the Spanish battle cry, "Santiago!" but he could not pull Atahualpa out of his litter, which was held aloft by what appeared to be important men. The Spaniards cut off the hands of several, but they continued to support the ruler's litter with their shoulders. As fast as each litter-bearer was killed, another took his place and was cut down in turn. Their loyal efforts were of no avail, however, for in the end they were all slain. Finally, seven or eight mounted Spaniards grabbed the edge of the litter, heaved against it, and turned it over on its side. Pizarro then took the captured Atahualpa to his camp.

Meanwhile, the terrible carnage continued in the square. One mass of Indians was pushed against a wall, which fortunately collapsed and allowed their escape into the plain beyond. Hundreds more were trampled to death, and the foot-soldiers set about those who remained in the square with such speed that in a relatively short time most of them had been put to the sword. During all of this, no Indian raised a weapon against a Spaniard, even when the cavalry jumped the broken wall and spread the slaughter among those who were fleeing. Long after night had fallen the horsemen were still lancing

natives in the fields, a slaughter that did not cease until a trumpet was sounded for the troops to reassemble at their camp.

The captured Inca monarch, informed of the terrible carnage, told his captors that one of the men they had killed in his litter was his steward, the lord of Chincha, of whom he was very fond. Among those who died with the steward were many of Atahualpa's counselors—so many that their names are unrecorded. Atahualpa's bodyguard was made up exclusively of important officials, and in killing them the conquistadores had struck a mortal blow at the administrative heart of the empire.

That night, in a chamber in Cajamarca, mighty Atahualpa, the New World's most powerful ruler, met his captor, the aged and bedraggled Francisco Pizarro. The bodies of thousands of the Inca's followers still lay in pools of blood in the square outside, and the air was filled with the groans of the wounded as the Inca confronted the few bearded ruffians who had seized him. Atahualpa asked whether the Spaniards were going to kill him, and they told him no, that Christians killed only in the impetuosity of the moment, not afterward.

In the wake of the slaughter both sides found themselves asking the same question: How could so powerful a monarch have been captured by a mere handful of adventurers? The answer was clear: Atahualpa had totally misjudged these invaders. His agents had reported that the Spaniards were few and disorganized, and the Inca never imagined that foreigners would be first to attack, especially with the odds overwhelmingly against them.

Pizarro and his men now had to decide on their next move. It was fortunate for them that Atahualpa was an absolute ruler and a semi-deity, for this meant that the Inca's orders would be obeyed even while he was held captive by a small force of foreigners. It also meant that Atahualpa's life was considered too precious for his armies to risk an attack that might cause his death. The conquest of Peru was thus unique in that it *began* with a checkmate. There were no preliminary contacts by traders or explorers, and the very first skirmish resulted in the capture of the monarch—an event that would normally have been the conquerors' final goal.

Pizarro arranged for the Inca's luxurious personal belongings and his serving women to be brought to him in captivity. Orders then went out—in the name of the Inca—notifying the army at Cajamarca to disband. Atahualpa's camp was promptly looted by the conquistadores. The Inca, observing that the Spaniards were most excited by objects of gold and silver, proposed that he should buy his freedom with the largest ransom ever paid. Pizarro asked the captive ruler how much he would be willing to pay, and how soon he could pay it. Atahualpa said he would give a room full of gold, a room the size of the one he was standing in—22 feet long by 17 feet wide. Touching a point roughly 8 feet up the wall, he indicated that the room would be filled to that point, and a white line was drawn around the chamber at that height. The Inca said he would fill the room to that level with gold objects—jars, pots, tiles, and other pieces—and then fill it twice more with silver. He agreed to complete this within two months. Paper and pen were hurriedly fetched, to record this extortionate ransom as though it were a legal agreement.

It eventually took six months to assemble this huge booty in a remote province of the empire. Atahualpa sent orders for all objects of gold and silver to be transported to Cajamarca, and soon long trains of llamas and native porters were winding along the Inca roads with these precious cargoes. One of the most sacred pre-Inca temples was at Pachacamac, in the coastal desert near modern Lima. The Incas had allowed this temple and oracle to continue to function as part of their official religion, but Atahualpa rightly suspected that its priests would refuse to part with their treasures to pay his ransom. He therefore advised Pizarro to send a contingent to ensure that Pachacamac was properly ransacked, and in January 1533 the conqueror's brother Hernando Pizarro set off for Pachacamac with a score of horsemen. They went with the Inca's protection, and they were the first Europeans to penetrate the Inca empire. Their mission was a failure, however, for although they overthrew the idol of Pachacamac, its priests refused to reveal where they had hidden their treasures.

Pachacamac was a minor setback, for the ransom from other areas began to arrive. One batch consisted of very large and remarkable pieces of gold including jars and pitchers of up to 50 pounds' capacity. Some Spaniards, whom Governor Pizarro had assigned to the task, began to crush these objects and to break them up so that the chamber would hold more. Seeing this Atahualpa asked,

"Why do you do that? I will give you so much gold that you will be satiated with it!" At the Inca's suggestion, Pizarro sent three Spaniards along hundreds of miles of Inca roads to supervise the collection of treasure from the capital city of Cuzco, and it was these men who personally prized the plates of gold from the holy sun temple Coricancha when scandalized natives refused to help.

The Spaniards in Cajamarca were waiting not only for the Inca's ransom to be accumulated but also for reinforcements to arrive. In the meantime they continued to assure Atahualpa that they sought nothing more than gold for themselves and their emperor. This was absolutely false, of course; they had always intended to remain in Peru as conquerors. Finally, at Easter 1533 assistance did reach Cajamarca in the form of Pizarro's original partner, Diego de Almagro, and a further 150 men. The Inca saw that he had been wrong to think he could buy the invaders off with treasure, treating the arrival of Almagro and his men as evidence that he was going to die. The arrival of reinforcements also spelled the death of the Inca's empire, for Pizarro now revealed his intention to distribute the peoples of the empire to serve individual conquistadores, who would found European-style towns.

By this time the chamber in Cajamarca was nearly filled with a priceless hoard of precious metals. Much of it consisted of vases, figures, jewelry, and personal ornaments, the masterpieces of Inca gold- and silver-smiths. Their destruction in the conquistadores' smelters was an irreparable artistic loss, although such a consideration apparently did not trouble the conquerors. On May 3 Francisco Pizarro had ordered his men to begin the enormous task of melting down more than 11 tons of gold objects and 26,000 pounds of silver. Native laborers were forced to toil over the furnaces, breaking up and crushing objects to be fed into them. On a good day the workers were able to melt down 600 pounds of metal, and in mid-June Hernando Pizarro set off for Spain with part of this booty, the so-called emperor's fifth. Pizarro took a few of the most magnificent objects intact, so that the Spanish monarch could admire their beauty. There were eighty-six such pieces, among them a silver urn shaped like an eagle, a golden idol the size of a four-year-old boy, drums, pitchers, and a replica of a stalk of maize, executed in gold and silver, from the famous "garden" of Coricancha.

Back in Cajamarca, the rest of Atahualpa's ransom was reduced to ingots, stamped with a royal mark, carefully weighed, and eventually distributed to the members of Pizarro's small force. Each horseman received the amazing total of 90 pounds of gold and 180 pounds of silver—enough to make each one of them a millionaire at current bullion prices. Foot-soldiers received half this quota; officers and royal officials received more, with Francisco Pizarro taking several times a horseman's share.

The distribution of the gold and silver took place on July 16, 1533. Pizarro had assured Atahualpa that he would be freed at this point to rule at least the northern part of his empire, and the Inca seemed to believe that this would indeed be the case. But when the time came, the Spaniards hesitated to release so powerful a ruler, insisting that Atahualpa should be exiled to Panama or Spain instead. Almagro's men, who had received none of the ransom treasure, wanted to push deeper into the Inca empire, and they wanted assurance that they would have a cut of any further booty. They also strongly urged that the Inca be killed. Atahualpa, they observed, had been deceived, and he could not be expected to remain a pliant puppet or to order his men not to attempt a rescue. The Inca now knew that the strangers could not be bought off with treasure, and that they were contemplating a full-scale invasion. The jittery kidnappers feared attack by an Inca army, and there was heated debate about their next move.

One evening only nine days after the distribution of the gold, an excited Spaniard rushed into Pizarro's chamber, dragging one of his Indian servants behind him. The latter insisted that he had seen a large Inca army approaching Cajamarca from the north. Hernando de Soto had already been sent out on a reconnaissance to investigate a similar rumor, and Pizarro decided not to await de Soto's return. Instead, swayed by Almagro's hard line and his own sense of panic, he authorized Atahualpa's execution. With the concurrence of the royal officials and his own officers, Pizarro decreed that the Inca had committed treason and sentenced him to death by burning—unless he should choose to convert to Christianity.

Atahualpa, for his part, argued that he had fulfilled his ransom, that with him in their power the Spaniards had nothing to fear, and that the rumor of an attack was unfounded. His eloquence was useless, however, and the Spaniards acted with chilling speed, as if fearful that a delay would produce evidence of the Inca's innocence. On the following evening—Saturday, July 26, 1533—Atahualpa was led out into the square and tied to the stake at which he was to be burned alive.

At this point Friar Vicente de Valverde explained that if the Inca accepted Christian baptism he would be killed by strangulation rather than by burning. As it happened, it was important in the Inca religion that a body remain intact after death, and Atahualpa—fully expected that his body would be mummified and worshiped as his ancestors' had been. Under the circumstances, strangulation was indeed preferable, and Atahualpa therefore accepted Valverde's offer of death by garrotting. Even in death Atahualpa was betrayed by the conquistadores, however, for they did not leave his body intact. "After he had been strangled in this way and the sentence executed," an eyewitness also recorded, "fire was thrown onto him to burn part of his clothing and flesh."

Another eyewitness recalled the behavior of the Incas on this grim occasion. "When he was taken out to be killed, all the native populace who were in the square, of whom there were many, prostrated themselves on the ground, letting themselves fall to the earth like drunken men." Pizarro decreed that there should be a Christian funeral to bury Atahualpa, with as much pomp as if he had been the most important Spaniard in the camp, and he himself wore a broad-brimmed black felt hat and was seen to weep at the funeral—for such was Spanish arrogance and hypocrisy.

VII

Conquest and Colonization

With Atahualpa dead, there was nothing to impede the Spanish advance into the Inca empire. Immediately after the burial of the slain ruler, Francisco Pizarro ordered all of the native chiefs to assemble in the central square of Cajamarca so that he could present them with a new ruler, one who would govern in the name of His Majesty, the king of Spain. Pizarro's puppet was Tupac Huallpa, a princeling from Huascar's line. The Spanish leader directed that the coronation should be carried out with as much ostentation as was possible, even though they were far from the imperial capital. The native chiefs were also required to perform an act of homage to the Spanish royal standard. Days of celebrations, games, and entertainments followed, and then, two weeks after the execution, Pizarro marched his men out of Cajamarca on the thousand-mile journey to Cuzco. The Spaniards were accompanied on this march by Atahualpa's old general Chalcuchima, by the new Inca, Tupac Huallpa, and by many officials who had been loyal to Huascar's Cuzco faction in the civil war and who were delighted by the fall of their enemy, Atahualpa.

While Pizarro marched south, news of Atahualpa's execution was carried back to Panama and, eventually, to Spain. The immediate reaction was highly critical. The governor of Panama praised Pizarro's conquest—"The riches and greatness of Peru increase daily to such an extent that they become almost impossible to believe . . . like something from a dream!"—but he was disgusted by the execution of the Inca. "In my opinion," he wrote, Atahualpa's guilt "should have been very

clearly established and proven, and there should have been no possible alternative whatever, before it became necessary to kill a man who had fallen into their hands and who had done no harm to any Spaniard or other person." The governor sensed where the true blame lay, for he knew that his countrymen's greed was virtually insatiable. The more the local leaders gave, he had found, the more the Spaniards tried to persuade their own officers and governors to kill and torture them to give more.

Perhaps anticipating such criticism, Pizarro wrote to Charles V that he had executed the Inca because Atahualpa had ordered "a mobilization of fighting men to come against us Christians." The monarch was skeptical, and he was also concerned about the sanctity of the notion of the divine right of kings. If an upstart adventurer like Pizarro could kill a powerful ruler with impunity, how safe was he? Therefore he sent this chilly reply to Pizarro: "We have been displeased by the death of Atahualpa, since he was a monarch, and particularly because it was done in the name of justice. . . . After being informed about the matter, we shall order what is necessary."

Pizarro and his men were far from the reach of royal censure, however, as they moved steadily down the Inca roads through the central Andes. Much of the populace welcomed the strangers or offered them no opposition: they were either supporters of Huascar's faction in the recent civil war or newly subjugated tribes that resented Inca rule. The Spaniards were by now well aware of both these destructive forces within the Inca empire, the

Beaker-shaped olla, or cooking pot, and fragments—all with spotted snake design.

one internecine and the other separatist. Both groups were too myopic to realize the terrible threat posed by this small band of invaders, and Pizarro naturally took full advantage of their naïveté by playing them off against one another.

The only real opposition to the Spanish advance came from garrisons of Atahualpa's army stationed in provincial capitals along the way. There was a skirmish at Chalcuchima's former base, Jauja, in which the Spaniards used their horses in combat for the first time—with devastating effect. In this and in all later battles, horses provided immense tactical superiority. On the march, the mounted invaders were often able to take native sentries by surprise; in actual fighting, the horses gave the Spaniards the double advantage of superior height and mobility.

At about the time of the Conquest of the Americas, a revolution in riding technique had occurred. Medieval knights had charged one another with legs outstretched to take up the shock of lance against armor. This posture was not necessary, of course, when one was fighting naked or lightly armed American Indians, and the conquistadores were able to adopt high Moorish saddles and ride with their legs doubled back, almost kneeling on the horse's back. The horses were trained to turn in response to the pressure of the reins on their necks, rather than the pull of those reins in their mouths. As a result they could be maneuvered easily and ridden with only one hand, leaving the other hand free for fighting, either with a long lance or a sword. A mounted man could use his horse to ride down

an enemy, and he was less exhausted when he arrived—inaccessible, and continually striking downward from his greater height.

Horses also had an immense psychological effect on the natives, for, as we have noted, they were unknown in the Americas. The Indians thought more of killing one of these animals than they did of killing ten men. If they killed a horse they often placed its head where the Spaniards would likely see it, decking it in flowers and branches as a sign of victory.

Firearms, by contrast, had little impact during the early phases of the Conquest. Cannon and arquebuses were cumbersome affairs that had to be fired with a lighted wick. When they did go off, their booming had a great effect but they killed few of the enemy. Much the same could be said for crossbows. These were developed in Europe to fire bolts with sufficient velocity to penetrate armor, but they were also cumbersome and had to be recocked with ratchets and pulleys. Moreover, they were unnecessary in any clash with unarmored Indians. Longbows would have been more effective, but they were not favored by the Spaniards.

In the mid-1500s the most deadly weapon in the European armory was still the sword. Toledan steel was famous, and Spanish swords were strong and supple—and kept razor-sharp by their owners. Spanish soldiers were considered the best swordsmen in Europe at this time, and those who crossed the Atlantic to make their fortunes in the Americas were the toughest and most adventurous. They were brave, ruthless, well-trained, fanatically greedy for the spoils of war, and sure of the rectitude of their religion and the superiority of their civilization.

Spanish fighting men of the sixteenth century had the added advantage of wearing armor. The richest among them possessed full suits of steel armor, with brilliantly articulated lames and hinges to allow every limb to move freely. But such protection was likewise unnecessary against natives armed with native weapons. Armor was also too hot for the coastal desert, too heavy for the high altitudes of the Andes, and too liable to rust in the humidity of a South American rainy season. The men involved in the Spanish Conquest therefore adopted a variety of substitutes: chain mail tunics; thick leather jerkins, boots, and aprons; and a form of ersatz armor, made of padded cotton and called *escaupil,* that they adopted from the Aztecs. Such protection was usually adequate to resist blows from Inca battle-axes or slingshots.

What did the Inca armies have to pit against this formidable weaponry? Very little, it seemed. Inca weapons were of biblical primitiveness. Their use of metals was unimaginative—stone shapes copied in bronze or copper—and their favorite forms were donut- or star-shaped mace heads and stubby swords fitted with sharp blades set along a wooden shaft. Ironically, Inca soldiers did not use the only weapon that the Spaniards really feared: arrows fired from longbows, and particularly arrows tipped with curare or other deadly poisons. The Incas' battle tactics were equally uninspired. In the early encounters of the Conquest, they regularly offered battle in the open, where Spanish horses could be deployed to devastating effect, and it was only from bitter experience that they learned to fight on rocky ground or steep slopes, where they would have the advantage. Although neither side recognized it, the Incas were physically adapted to life at high altitudes, where they could run and fight with greater agility and endurance than the breathless and exhausted Europeans, and it is interesting to speculate on what the outcome of Pizarro's expedition might have been if the Incas had consistently lured the invaders to battle sites high in the Andes.

The Incas were also at a psychological disadvantage in combatting the Spanish. They knew nothing about the origin, experience, culture, or intentions of the strange people who had appeared so suddenly in their midst, and it was altogether natural that they should be awed by and fearful of the Spaniards and their horses. The Andean peasantry was by nature docile and respectful—and the Spaniards exhibited a commanding self-assurance. For a people as religious and superstitious as the Peruvians, there may even have been a strong apprehension that they were actually fighting a race of gods. After all, the Inca creation legend itself declared that after making the world and its creatures, the creator-god Viracocha disappeared over the waters of the Pacific, westward toward the setting sun. He told his companions that he would eventually return to them, and having said this, he strode to sea with his two servants, moving across the water as if it were land, without sinking. Pizarro's men had in fact reached Peru from that same Pacific shore, raising the suspicion that they

116

Its colors were braver and its cut-work and embroidery intact four centuries ago, but it is still possible to make out the salient details of Governor Francisco Pizarro's personal battle standard. The central escutcheon, shown below, encircles a crest composed of the royal lions of Leon and the castles of Castile—which might, in light of Pizarro's achievements, be more rightly identified as the puma of Cuzco and the ramparts of Sacsayhuaman.

were the returning Viracocha, and so for centuries after the Conquest, Peruvian Indians addressed all white men as "Viracocha." Intelligent or educated Incas had no such illusions; they quickly recognized the invaders as brutal and unscrupulous mortals. But the rapid and effortless capture of the divine Atahualpa shook even their confidence, and ordinary Peruvian soldiers, fighting on foot against mounted, armored conquistadores, must have suffered terrible uncertainty indeed.

Pizarro's force paused at Jauja after its first successful battle against Atahualpa's army. There the Spaniards were welcomed by the local people for two reasons: because they had dislodged Atahualpa's northern army, which had recently captured Jauja from Huascar's faction; and because Jauja was in territory once held by the Huanca tribe, many of whose members resented Inca domination. While at Jauja, Pizarro declared the town the capital of Spanish Peru. Members of his party used the stopover to rest themselves and their horses, and to write their wills in anticipation of the final advance toward Cuzco. During their stay in Jauja the puppet Inca Tupac Huallpa died mysteriously, possibly poisoned by Chalcuchima or others loyal to the memory of Atahualpa.

Because Pizarro left some men to garrison Jauja, he marched south with only 130 men, 100 of whom were mounted. He soon split his force, sending the 70 best horsemen ahead under Hernando de Soto. This dashing commander was charged with capturing bridges and stores, which he generally succeeded in doing. Atahualpa's men had destroyed many bridges and food stores as they retreated, but the supporters of Huascar had hidden building materials and had sequestered reserves of food.

Soto occupied the next important Inca city, Vilcashuamán, by riding so fast that Inca scouts, traveling on foot, did not have time to warn of his approach. His horsemen also won a hard-fought skirmish in the central plaza and side streets of Vilcashuamán. At this point Soto's party decided to disobey Pizarro's express orders and push ahead toward the Inca capital. Soto left a letter in which he explained that he was moving forward to prevent the conjunction of two of Atahualpa's armies, but one of Soto's men, Diego de Trujillo, admitted that the reason for this insubordination was that "since we had endured the hardships, we should enjoy the entry into Cuzco without the reinforcements that were coming behind." By "enjoy the entry" he meant that Soto's hotheads wanted to be the first to loot the imperial capital.

On November 8 Soto's men managed to cross the last great obstacle before Cuzco—the deep canyon of the Apurímac River. The Inca road crossed the Apurímac on a famous suspension bridge (later immortalized by Thornton Wilder in *The Bridge of San Luis Rey*), but Atahualpa's army had destroyed it. By yet another stroke of good fortune, the year 1533 was a particularly dry one and the conquistadores were therefore able to ford this great river.

As the invaders toiled up the far bank of the canyon, advancing single file and leading their horses, Inca soldiers suddenly appeared over the brow of the hill and charged down on the weary and unprepared Spaniards. The dreaded horses were exhausted and their riders could scarcely raise them to a trot—and some not even to a walk. Thus encouraged, the Indians attacked with great fury. Five Spaniards were killed in the ensuing fighting, and almost all the rest were wounded. As night fell, Soto's men huddled on a hillock, surrounded by the Inca army and understandably frightened.

With extraordinary prescience, Pizarro had split his force again some four days earlier and had sent more of his horsemen to overtake Soto. As this group pressed forward, they learned about the battle on the slope above the Apurímac. Advancing through the night, the relief force sounded a trumpet that was heard by Soto's beleaguered men, and the two groups combined in the darkness. The following morning they were able to force a passage through the Inca army.

Shaken by this near-disaster, Soto paused at the top of the Apurímiac canyon to await his commander, Pizarro. Soon after the Spanish force was reunited, they received an unexpected visitor: a young Inca prince called Manco, one of the very few survivors of Atahualpa's massacre of Huascar's branch of the royal family. This important prince had been a fugitive from Atahualpa's men, and he came to the Spanish alone, looking like a common Indian. Pizarro welcomed Manco as a convenient new puppet, and in exchange Manco may have revealed that the doughty old general Chalcuchima had instigated the recent attacks on the Spanish column. In any event Pizarro certainly suspected Chalcuchima of this, as well as of poisoning the previous puppet,

Tupac Huallpa. Pizarro accused Chalcuchima of these crimes and had him tied to a stake. The aged warrior proudly refused conversion to Christianity, and as he died in the flames he called on the god Viracocha and on his fellow commander, Quisquis, to avenge his death.

Chalcuchima's plea was in vain, however, for Quisquis and the last remnants of Atahualpa's army had been demoralized by their monarch's death. They offered fierce resistance to the Spaniards at the edge of Cuzco, but when the Europeans won yet again, Quisquis retreated to the mountains and eventually led his army hundreds of miles northward toward Quito. His departure left the Inca capital undefended, and most of its citizens welcomed the arrival of the Spaniards and their new puppet Inca, Manco. At the first light on November 15, Pizarro drew up the infantry and cavalry and prepared to enter Cuzco. His men were arrayed in careful battle order and on the alert, for they were sure that the enemy would launch an attack on them along the road. But no soldiers appeared, and they entered the city with no further fighting.

Pizarro marched his men along the straight, clean streets of the Inca city, marveling at the efficiency of Cuzco's masonry and the channeled watercourses that drained its streets. The invaders moved directly to the ceremonial heart of the capital, and Pizarro lodged his officers in the palaces of the dead Inca rulers. Because these palaces were kept intact by each ruler's descendants, as we have noted, the conquistadores were able to install themselves amid fine tapestries and use the table service of deceased

monarchs. A few weeks later the citizens of Cuzco staged a customarily lavish coronation for the new Inca. Manco was crowned with the scarlet fringe and seated on the Inca's plumed throne during thirty days of feasting, chanting, sacrifices, processions, and drinking.

The Spaniards used Manco's coronation to force the native leaders into acts of submission to the throne of Spain. As Pizarro's secretary noted, both sides thought they had achieved a victory, but the situation remained tense and ambiguous. Pizarro performed yet another ceremony, "founding" the Inca capital as a Spanish municipality. The act of foundation was done on a gibbet that symbolized Spanish justice and power, and from that bloody pulpit Pizarro made his declaration.

The conquistadores were now free to enjoy the fruits of their victory, and they promptly set about plundering Cuzco. It was one of those infrequent moments in history when a gang of unscrupulous conquerors loot at will the capital of a great empire. In the words of one of the participants, "some of them immediately began to dismantle the walls of the temple that were of gold and silver; others to dig up jewels and gold vases that were with the dead; others to seize idols of the same materials. They sacked the houses and the fortress, which still contained much of Huayna Capac's gold. In short, they took a greater quantity of gold and silver there than they had in Cajamarca with the capture of Atahualpa." One group of Spaniards went to the sun temple Coricancha, whose high priest was appalled at this sacrilege and shouted, "How dare

·THE·RICHE·MINᵭES·OF·POTOSSI·

THE
DISCOVERIE AND CONQVEST
of the Prouinces of *PERV*, and
the Nauigation in the South
Sea, along that Coast.
And also of the ritche Mines
of *POTOSI*.

you enter here! Anyone who enters here must fast for a year beforehand, and must enter barefoot and bearing a load!" The looters paid no attention to what he said, however, and entered the sacred enclosure. Most of its contents were still intact, including many golden llamas, figurines, pitchers, and other objects, and the Spaniards set to pillaging.

All of Cuzco's treasures were ultimately melted down, yielding more than 2½ tons of gold and 51½ tons of good-to-poor-quality silver. This was duly stamped with the royal mark and distributed among the lucky adventurers after the royal fifth had been sent to Spain.

During the year after Pizarro's entry into Cuzco, Manco tried to rule as Inca in the traditional manner. Inca officials moved out across the empire to repair the ravages of the recently concluded civil war and to reassert central authority over rebellious tribes. Pizarro's Spaniards had different views, however. To them, Peru was a conquered nation and they were its new masters.

In the forty years since Spaniards had first settled in the Americas, they had devised a system that both rewarded the conquistadores and sought to persuade them to remain in the New World. Each soldier was awarded an *encomienda*, or control over a designated group of natives—usually people living in a defined region or subjects of a single chief. A Spaniard did not technically own the land in his *encomienda*, but he could extort undefined amounts of tribute from its wretched people. These people paid the *encomienda*-holder assessments in the form of animals, food products, rope, saddles, timber, metal, utensils, and implements, not to mention personal service as porters, herdsmen, farmers, or household servants. The *encomienda*-holder, in turn, was expected to live in one of the Spanish municipalities, which were often Inca towns "founded" anew as Spanish ones. This was done for defensive reasons, so that the conquerors would be united, not scattered about their new estates, and also to protect the natives from direct abuse. In practice, however, absentee *encomienda*-holders generally appointed brutal overseers to collect their tribute, which their Indian subjects had to carry on their backs to the Spaniards' residence in town.

This tribute, which had formerly gone into state storehouses as provision against years of famine, now went to the personal treasury of a foreign master. It was, of course, a few years before Peru felt the full impact of this monstrous new system. In the first few years of the Conquest the Peruvians were only vaguely aware that the strangers regarded themselves as conquerors, that many more of them were pouring into the country, and that they intended to stay forever. During that initial period, before the Conquest was fully consolidated, the Spaniards dared not behave with unbridled excess. Their first concern, as we have noted, was gold and silver, and they were willing to do anything to obtain these precious metals. Native chiefs were tortured to make them reveal the whereabouts of real or supposed treasures, and the chronicles are full of accounts of chiefs being burned alive, savaged by trained hunting dogs, or subjected to rope torture of the genitals.

Spanish adventurers generally sailed to the New World without their women, and it was inevitable, therefore, that those who reached Peru should procure native women for sexual purposes, just as they procured native men as porters and laborers. At first, the women were flattered to be chosen by these godlike strangers, and their fathers acquiesced out of hospitality. But with the arrival of more Europeans and with the removal of earlier restraints, the demands of the conquerors began to undermine native society. In the words of one observer, from this time onward the Peruvians "adopted the custom of having public prostitutes and abandoned their former practice of marrying—for no woman who was good-looking was safe to her husband; it would be a miracle if she escaped the Spaniards. . . ."

The convents of *mamaconas* were early victims of Spanish licentiousness. We have already seen how, before the Spaniards met Atahualpa at Cajamarca, Hernando de Soto allowed his men to rape the chosen women at Cajas in the northern mountains. As the Inca state system collapsed, these convents were dispersed. Hiram Bingham would later argue that some of the women fled to Machu Picchu. His theory was based on the fact that a majority of the hundred-odd skeletons his excavators found in Machu Picchu's tombs seemed to be those of women, and that many female clothing pins and spindle whorls were excavated in the ruins. But there is no further evidence to support Bingham's idea. Indeed, little at Machu Picchu indicates that the town was occupied after the Spanish Conquest, and the female remains are most likely those of chosen women who lived and worked at Machu Picchu in far earlier times.

Spanish abuse of native women even extended to members of the royal family. Pizarro, a bachelor in his mid-fifties, took a teen-aged Inca princess as his concubine and was reportedly delighted when she bore him a daughter. He later arranged for this girl and his children born to another princess to be legitimized, but he refused to marry either of the mothers. Some conquistadores did marry natives, but most felt that such permanent unions were beneath them—this despite the fact that Pizarro's men were social upstarts and their consorts were native aristocracy. Manco Inca's son later described an incident that typified the behavior of the conquerors. Gonzalo Pizarro, youngest of the four Pizarro brothers, conceived a passion for the Inca's sister, Cura Ocllo. This scandalized Manco and his officials, for she shared the Inca's semi-divinity. The high priest therefore rebuked Gonzalo Pizarro, whose reply was typically boorish: "How dare you talk like that to the King's official? Don't you know what sort of men we Spaniards are? By the King's life, if you don't shut up I'll catch you and play games with you and your friends that you'll remember all your lives. I swear that if you don't keep quiet I'll slit you open, alive, and make little pieces of you!"

To avoid such an incident the Indians produced another girl, one who looked like the royal princess. She was brought out, beautifully arrayed, and Gonzalo Pizarro, apparently deceived, shouted, "Mr. Manco Inca, if she is for me, give her to me right

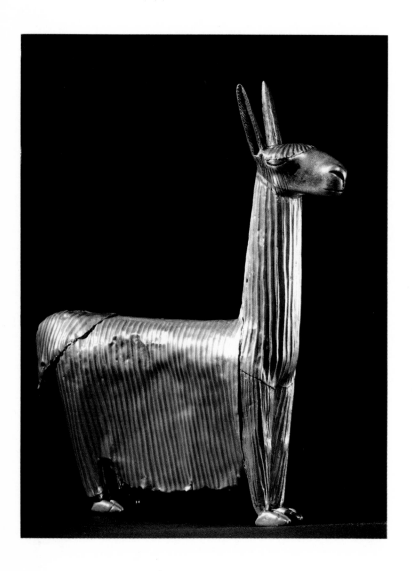

away for I cannot bear to wait!" He then went up to her and, oblivious to all else, kissed and embraced her as if she were his legitimate wife. Manco and the rest were amazed and laughed at this, but the girl was horrified at being embraced by a stranger. She screamed like a madwoman, averring that she would run away rather than have anything to do with people like these. But Manco ordered the girl to comply and she went.

The first two years after Manco's coronation were a honeymoon period between the young Inca and the foreigners who had helped him to the throne. During these months more Spaniards sailed to Peru, all intent on enriching themselves at the expense of the natives. These were adventurers as tough and brutal as the villains of any American Western, and from them Manco and his advisers came to realize the true nature of the invaders. Pizarro's small expedition was turning into a permanent occupation, and with the distribution of valleys and chiefdoms as *encomiendas* the empire was being engulfed in a system of massive personal tribute.

Manco and his officials watched in horror as the Spaniards imposed their will on the Inca empire. A senior Franciscan, describing this process, noted that "the injuries and injustices that have been done to the poor docile Indians cannot be counted. Everything from the very beginning is injury. Their liberty has been removed; their nobles have lost their nobility, authority and all forms of jurisdiction; and the Spaniards have stolen their pastures and many fine lands, and imposed intolerable tributes on them."

At the height of the encomienda *abuses the tribute extracted annually from one of Peru's poorest provinces included 400 ounces of gold and silver; 640 bushels of wheat, 1,280 of barley, 320 of maize, and 160 of potatoes; 30 pigs, 300 birds, and 30 llamas. Under this prodigious burden the nation's reserve stores were soon depleted and its food distribution system, which had long provided for the people's wants even in the leanest years, simply collapsed. Llamas (right, below) and their small cousins the alpacas (left, below), once raised principally as wool-bearing beasts of burden, were now consumed wholesale by famished Indians.*

VIII

The Search for Vilcabamba

Manco Inca had two main reasons for ending his collaboration with the Spanish expeditionary force, headed by Francisco Pizarro, which had landed on his empire's Pacific shores five years earlier. The first of these was Diego de Almagro's Chilean expedition, a venture that temporarily removed many of the conquistadores from Peru. The Inca high priest, Villac Umu, who accompanied this expedition, witnessed its brutality firsthand. He grew increasingly alarmed by the Spaniards' behavior, and before the Chilean expedition was six months old he escaped and made his way back to Cuzco, where he sought to persuade his young relative Manco to take action against the invaders.

The second cause of Manco's change of heart was direct insults to the Inca himself. Pizarro had left his uncouth young brothers, Juan and Gonzalo, in charge of Cuzco while he busied himself founding the new coastal town that later became modern Peru's capital, Lima. No sooner had Francisco departed than the young Pizarros began to abuse Manco Inca, demanding still more treasure from the puppet ruler. By this time, of course, Cuzco had been largely denuded of its treasure; what remained were vague rumors of vast hordes of gold and silver, buried by the Incas in advance of the Spaniards' arrival. These were, however, figments of the conquistadores' avaricious imaginations; moreover, Manco Inca, mindful of Atahualpa's fate, would surely have known that their existence would not have protected him anyway.

Soon after the return of Villac Umu, Manco slipped out of Cuzco, possibly to begin rallying sup-

port for a military campaign against the invaders. He was quickly recaptured, and from a report by Manco's son we know that "Gonzalo Pizarro ordered his men to bring irons and a chain, with which they shackled my father as they pleased. They thrust a chain around his neck and irons on his feet." Manco himself later recalled that, although he gave quantities of golden objects to his tormentors, "they called me a dog and struck me, and took my wives and the lands that I farmed. . . . They said to me: 'Dog, give us gold! If not, you will be burned.' "

The wretched royal captive's great opportunity came in April 1536. The older Pizarro brother, Hernando, had returned to Cuzco and rashly released the young Inca, who promised to fetch a gold statue of one of his ancestors from the Yucay valley, northeast of Cuzco. But Manco went instead to the hills beyond the Yucay valley. He had already sent emissaries to all parts of the empire, and great levies of native troops were even then converging on Cuzco. All this had been achieved without the knowledge of the Spanish invaders, for the efficient imperial apparatus was still functioning despite the recent civil war and and foreign invasion, and it was still possible for native armies to be provisioned, armed, mobilized, and given marching orders, all in complete secrecy.

A reconnaissance by Spanish cavalry first sighted Manco's levies assembling in the Yucay valley. These horsemen hurried back to warn Hernando Pizarro, but as they returned they observed squadrons of Indian warriors arriving and camping in

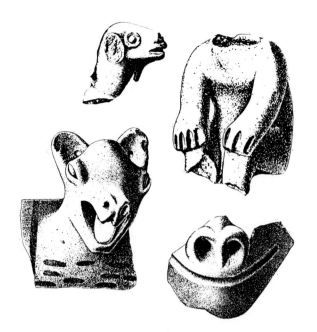

From top: trunk and arms of figurine, dish handles in shape of dog and goat heads, and shard in form of monkey.

the steepest places around Cuzco, presumably to await the assembly of all their forces. So many troops came that they covered the fields, resembling a 1½-mile black carpet around the city.

There were only 190 Spaniards in the besieged capital, and of these only 80 had horses. This vastly outnumbered force was supported by native auxiliaries drawn from anti-Inca tribes and from branches of the royal family opposed to Manco. Throughout the first weeks of the siege, Inca forces continued to arrive, and the high priest Villac Umu, in command of the siege operations, contented himself with the occupation of Sacsayhuaman and the construction of barricades and pits designed to immobilize the conquistadores' horses.

Manco's attack came on Saturday, May 6, 1936. Hundreds of warriors rushed down the steep slope from Sacsayhuaman and entered the city's narrow lanes while others fought their way from the surrounding countryside. The Spaniards had barricaded themselves in the royal palaces and enclosures that stood alongside the main square, and one eyewitness recalled that "the Indians supported one another most effectively, thinking that it was all over. They charged through the streets with the greatest determination and fought hand-to-hand with the Spaniards."

Cuzco's houses and palaces were all roofed in thatch, which the natives decided to set on fire, sacrificing their capital city to rout the detested Spanish. They therefore heated the shots for their slingshots and wrapped them in burning cotton. The thatch roofs caught fire and began burning

fiercely before the Spaniards realized how it was being done. There was a strong wind that day, and it seemed at one time that the city was one great sheet of flame. The Indians were shouting loudly and there were clouds of smoke so dense that the Spaniards could neither hear nor see one another. The whole of Cuzco burned in one day, producing acrid smoke that almost suffocated the Spaniards and caused them great suffering. Luckily for Pizarro's men, one side of the square consisted of unroofed enclosures, and they huddled there, under a withering barrage from slingshots and javelins.

With Cuzco's thatched roofs burned away the natives could run along the tops of the house walls and were, for once, above the dreaded horses in the streets below. After six days of fierce fighting the Indians had recaptured almost all of the city; the Spaniards held only the main square and a few houses around it. The conquistadores, who could see no hope of relief from any direction and did not know what to do, were extremely frightened. Some wanted to abandon the city and make the desperate journey to the coast across hundreds of miles of mountain roads. Others felt that their only hope lay in recapturing Sacsayhuaman, the temple-fortress that overlooked Cuzco, from which the natives had launched their most effective attacks.

Indian observers noted that the Spaniards spent the whole of one night on their knees and with their hands clasped in prayer. The following morning, very early, they emerged from the enclosure and mounted their horses as if they were going to fight. They suddenly put spurs to their horses and, despite the enemy, set off at full gallop through an opening in the siege defenses and charged off up the hillside at breakneck speed.

This squadron consisted of fifty horsemen, the majority of those left in the city, and it was led by Juan Pizarro. The desperate Spaniards forced their way up the main highway, with native auxiliaries bravely filling in the pits and holes that had been dug to catch the horses' hooves. Manco's men kept up a heavy fire, but they could not stop this contingent from reaching the plateau above Cuzco, or, once there, from racing along the highway and then wheeling behind some hills to reach the parade ground at the foot of Sacsayhuaman'sramparts.

Days of heavy fighting ensued. Pizarro's horsemen broke through barriers that the natives had erected near the temple walls, and fought hand-to-hand amid the rocky outcrops opposite them. Whenever the riders approached the walls they were driven back by slingshot and javelin fire. Late one afternoon, Juan Pizarro attempted to charge the main gate. He had been wounded on the jaw the previous day and consequently was not wearing his steel helmet. He was struck on the head by a missile hurled from the salient rampart, and the blow proved fatal. The governor's brother was carried down to Cuzco in secret—and buried at night so the Indians would not know he was dead.

The following day the Indians counterattacked repeatedly. Hernando Pizarro sent in twelve of his remaining horsemen, but Manco Inca also sent reinforcements. The Spaniards, however, had been making siege ladders, and as night fell they used these to launch an assault that succeeded in taking parts of the great terraced walls. The defenders retreated into the maze of towers at the top of the temple, followed by one dashing Spaniard who performed feats worthy of a silent-screen hero. Under a hail of missiles he climbed a scaling rope and stepped off from the tower wall, parrying missiles with his shield. He squeezed through a window, hurled himself at the Indians inside, and finally emerged at the top of a tower, from which vantage he encouraged his men to assault it.

On the Indian side there was a heroic defense led by an Inca noble, a warrior who had acquired a Spanish sword and helmet but continued to wield a native shield and battle-axe. He strode about the tower at its topmost level, repulsing any Spaniards who tried to mount with scaling ladders and killing any Indians who tried to surrender by smashing their heads with his battle-axe and hurling them from the top of the tower. Although he received two arrow wounds, he kept on fighting.

Eventually the Spaniards attacked with four simultaneous scaling ladders, their assault supported by many native allies. They gradually gained the advantage. As Inca resistance crumbled the gallant nobleman who had led the defense of the castle hurled weapons down on the attackers in a frenzy of despair. He grabbed handfuls of earth and scoured his face in anguish, covered his head in his cloak, and then leaped to his death from the top of the temple-fortress. The remaining Indians soon gave way, and Hernando Pizarro and his men were able to enter—whereupon they put all 1,500

of those inside to the sword. Those who escaped did so by jumping from the walls, and there were heaps of corpses on the cliff above Cuzco. The coat-of-arms later awarded to Cuzco commemorated this grisly scene with its orle banded by eight condors, the great vulture-like birds that are said to have descended to eat the slaughtered natives when the castle fell to the Spaniards.

The capture of Sacsayhuaman was the turning point in the siege. Hernando Pizarro's men remained trapped in Cuzco for ten more months, but they were too well protected to be destroyed. Manco's army, on the other hand, was composed largely of farmers, who had to return to their crops. Although there were many more battles and skirmishes, neither side could break the deadlock—even despite the fact that other native rebellions had destroyed all of the isolated pockets of Spaniards in other parts of Peru. From his new capital, Lima, Francisco Pizarro's forces easily repulsed an attack by another Inca army, but the three relief expeditions he sent into the mountains in a bid to help his brothers in Cuzco were all annihilated by Manco's troops, each group being trapped in a mountain defile and crushed under volleys of boulders and missiles from the surrounding slopes. In the end, Cuzco was relieved by the return of Almagro's Chilean expedition, which staggered back across the desolate Atacama desert and reached the beleaguered city in April 1537.

There were several subsequent attempts to win Manco Inca back to serve under Spanish rule, but the Inca was too proud to consent—and too aware

The de Bry at right, which shows natives pouring molten gold down the throats of their Spanish masters, is what can only be described as wishful thinking—an Indian revenge fantasy as interpreted by a Flemish painter who never saw Peru. In truth, the Incas who did not follow Manco into the deep forests of the Vilcabamba led lives of unremitting hardship—"the most wretched and miserable lives of any people on earth," according to a sympathetic senior official of sixteenth-century Peru.

of Spanish perfidy to surrender. He decided instead to retreat to a more inaccessible part of Peru, there to continue the struggle against the foreign invaders. In July 1537 a meeting of Inca chiefs was held at the fortified temple complex of Ollantaytambo, located on the Urubamba River midway between Cuzco and Machu Picchu. It was an emotional moment, for Manco and his advisers knew that he was being forced to abandon the home of his ancestors, to leave the open, hilly homelands of the Incas and retreat into the forests of Vilcabamba. Villac Umu led the prayers, sacrifices, and lamentations as the Inca and the sacred idols were prepared for transportation to the new refuge.

Manco Inca retreated down a valley which lay behind the mountains that flank the east bank of the Urubamba. He then recrossed the river on a strategic suspension bridge and ascended a tributary to reach the town of Vitcos. This route bypassed Machu Picchu altogether—the "lost city" having apparently been rejected in favor of a section of the Vilcabamba region farther from Spanish-occupied Cuzco. Because the ridge-top city of Machu Picchu stood high above the difficult granite gorges of the Urubamba, inaccessible to all but the most agile, it was not used by Manco and his followers and it was never discovered by the various Spanish parties that ventured into the Vilcabamba area to negotiate with—or attack—Manco and his successors. All those expeditions used the valley route east of the Urubamba or approached Vilcabamba from the southwest, across the swift-flowing Apurímac River (see diagram, page 38).

The first attack on Manco came soon after his flight. Immediately after reoccupying Cuzco, Almagro sent his most dashing officer, the Jewish-born Rodrigo Orgóñez, to attempt to capture the fugitive Inca. Orgóñez moved rapidly up country, passing the obstacles and broken bridges left by the retreating Indians. He took Vitcos by surprise and captured great quantities of llamas and stores—and even some members of the Inca's family. He failed to catch Manco himself, however; the Inca was spirited away in the arms of his faithful runners and survived in the jungle until Orgóñez departed. Although Manco continued to use the town and lodgings at Vitcos after Orgóñez's raid, he decided that he must build another, less vulnerable refuge. His remaining followers built a new town called Vilcabamba City, two days' march from Vitcos but in a far less accessible location.

In 1539, two years after the collapse of his first rising, Manco Inca made another heroic attempt to drive the Spanish invaders from the Inca empire. He and members of his family traveled secretly through Spanish-occupied Peru, sounding a call to rebellion. Their summons was not always successful: some tribes, among them the Huanca of the central Andes, were too blind to the dangers of Spanish rule to heed this call and ally themselves with the Inca. Others sensed that Manco's attempt was hopeless; having failed to dislodge the Spaniards in 1537, he could not possibly hope to do so now that hundreds more of them had entered the country. Despite this, the appeal had some success, with large parts of Peru reverting to Inca rule and many con-

128

tingents of Spaniards suffering defeat. There was particularly severe fighting in the Bolivian altiplano beyond Lake Titicaca and in the mountains of northern Peru, but in the end Spanish weapons, horses, and fighting skills prevailed. One by one, Manco's commanders were defeated or surrendered. Even Villac Umu capitulated after conducting a bold but futile guerrilla campaign in the mountains southwest of Cuzco.

All that remained outside Spanish control after this second rebellion was Manco Inca's own stronghold in Vilcabamba, and a large expedition was mounted under Gonzalo Pizarro to capture it. Pizarro entered the Vilcabamba region by the usual route, bypassing Machu Picchu, and ascended the Vilcabamba valley to a point, beyond Vitcos, where his 300 men had to leave their horses and continue on foot along jungle trails. In one defile Manco's men had prepared a breastwork, piling boulders on the hillside in front of it. Their ambush was launched slightly too soon, however, and killed only 36 Spaniards, although it did force Gonzalo to retreat for a time with his many wounded men. Ten days later, he returned with reinforcements and managed to outflank the breastwork. Gonzalo's men continued to a plain beyond, where Manco Inca purportedly had his residence. It was the Spaniards' first sight of the Inca's new refuge, Vilcabamba. Once again the Inca himself had eluded their grasp, his runners spiriting him away again just as the Spanish forces were entering the city. And although Gonzalo Pizarro remained in the area for two months and sent many expeditions to search for

him, Manco managed to hide successfully among the tribes of the Amazonian rain forest.

With the failure of this second campaign by a leading conquistador, Vilcabamba gained a fearsome reputation. Spaniards who had been there were appalled by the difficulties encountered in traversing the jungle-clad mountains, and Hernando Pizarro wrote the king that "great resources would be needed to penetrate that land. It could be done only with very heavy expenditure, and since those who went there could not afford this, their enthusiasm came to an end."

Governor Francisco Pizarro, for his part, was furious at the expedition's failure to capture Manco, and he vented his fury on the Inca high priest and other commanders who had surrendered after the recent rising. He first lured them down to the Yucay valley on the pretext of awarding them lands there, and then, once they had arrived, sentenced sixteen of them without trial and burned them alive. He also persecuted Manco's young sister, Cura Ocllo, who had been captured in Vilcabamba. Cieza de León recorded that both Pizarro and his secretary had intercourse with her, after which she was stripped, tied to a stake, beaten by anti-Inca natives, and shot to death with arrows. In the midst of these tortures she reportedly called out to her persecutors, "Hurry up and put an end to me, so that your appetites may be fully satisfied!" Beyond this she endured her martyrdom in silence. To add to this cruelty, Pizarro had her body floated down the river in a basket in the hope that it would be found by Manco's followers.

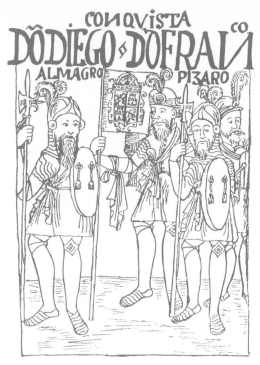

Manco Inca was left undisturbed at Vitcos and Vilcabamba for six years, becoming in this period a true guerrilla leader, harassing Spanish communications along the Lima-Cuzco road and surprising isolated groups of Spanish soldiers and travelers. The conquistadores were now preoccupied with quarrels of their own, for Pizarro and his original partner, Almagro, had fallen out over which of them was entitled to govern Cuzco. The result was three civil wars. In the first, the Pizarros defeated and executed Almagro; in the second, which broke out in 1541, Almagro's followers assassinated Francisco Pizarro in Lima and gained temporary control of all Peru; and in the third, a year later, a royal army regained the country from the Almagrists.

Manco had always had more sympathy for Almagro, and he understandably regarded the Pizarros as his deadly enemies. He therefore gave sanctuary to five Almagrist fugitives who fled to the Vilcabamba region after their faction was defeated in 1542, and he proved to be a good host. He lodged his guests at Vitcos, and he often dined with them or joined them in games. In return, they taught Manco's men Spanish fighting methods, thereby gaining the Inca's trust. Once again this trust was misplaced, however, for when the five rebels decided to return to Spanish-occupied territory in 1545 they thought they would enjoy a better reception if they first killed the Inca. They therefore attacked Manco and then escaped from Vitcos on horseback. A contingent of Inca troops was able to catch and kill the traitors, but Manco died of the wounds he had received.

Manco Inca left three young sons, and after a twelve-year regency they succeeded him as rulers in Vilcabamba. They and their officials made fewer raids into Spanish Peru, wanting only to be left in peace in the tiny state of Vilcabamba. In those few valleys and forested hills lingered a last reminder of the lost grandeur of the Inca empire. The existence of this unconquered enclave served as an inspiration to the mass of Peruvians, on whom the full weight of Spanish oppression now fell. Forced labor was applied on a massive scale in the silver and mercury mines that had been established in Peru, with thousands of Indians being marched cross-country to toil in the dark and dangerous pits.

The Spanish authorities were naturally eager to complete their conquest by eliminating the Vilcabamba state, and having failed by military means, they tried diplomacy. A number of embassies were sent into Vilcabamba, each accompanied by some member of the Inca royal family, many of whom were living under Spanish rule. These envoys left detailed reports of their journeys, and Manco's second son, Titu Cusi Yupanqui, also dictated a remarkable autobiographical memoir. During the 1560s, some Christian friars were permitted to enter Vilcabamba to preach, and they too left accounts of what they saw in the remote Inca state.

Spanish diplomacy succeeded in luring one of Manco's sons out of Vilcabamba in 1559, but this did not put an end to the small state, for the Inca's brother ruled there in his absence. After resisting Spanish blandishments for more than a decade, Titu Cusi died unexpectedly in 1571, apparently of a stroke, and he was succeeded by a reclusive younger brother, Tupac Amaru. This new Inca and his generals wanted to revert to a traditional Inca existence and to break all contacts with Spanish Peru, a reaction that coincided with the arrival in Peru of a tough new viceroy, Francisco de Toledo. Toledo tried to continue the diplomatic dialogue with Vilcabamba, but he grew increasingly angry when his embassies were rebuffed. The last straw came when a prominent Spanish envoy was killed by Vilcabamba border guards; Viceroy Toledo decided that Vilcabamba must be conquered.

An enormous expedition was launched against the tiny Inca state, with heavily armed contingents of Spaniards entering Vilcabamba by three different routes. There was one battle as the invaders moved up the Vilcabamba River valley, and another a few weeks later as Toledo's men marched into the forests around the city itself. The remnants of Manco Inca's forces could do nothing against such opposition, and attempts to stop the advance with boulders came to nothing. And so, on Thursday, June 24, 1572, the viceroy's men moved into Vilcabamba—all on foot, for the wild and rugged country was unsuitable for horses. Within, the attackers found that some four hundred houses, various native shrines and temples, and the Inca's palace had all been sacked so effectively that, had the Spaniards and their Indian auxiliaries done it, the destruction could not have been more complete. All the Indians had fled, taking whatever provisions they could with them. The rest they burned, and when the invaders arrived the storehouses were still smoking.

One member of the expedition described the Vilcabamba region as having a tropical climate, with an abundance of such hot lowland foods as manioc, sweet potatoes, cotton, coca, guavas, pineapples, avocado pears, and sugar cane. He reported that "the town has, or rather had, a location half a league [about 1½ miles] wide, rather like the plan of Cuzco but covering a longer distance in length." This description is important to us, for it scarcely corresponds to the plan of Machu Picchu, which is a compact place on a sharp ridge, not a sprawling place in a broad valley like Cuzco's. Nor would Machu Picchu produce the profusion of tropical forest foods that were found in Vilcabamba. Another important passage in the soldier's chronicle describes Manco's palace, burned by the Incas in 1572: "The house and halls were covered in good thatch. The Incas had a palace on different levels, covered in roof tiles, and with the entire palace painted with a great variety of paintings in their style—something well worth seeing."

The natives of Vilcabamba hoped to repeat Manco's escapes of 1537 and 1539, and they therefore hurried off into the depths of the jungle with Manco's son, the Inca Tupac Amaru. This time, however, they underestimated Spanish determination: a series of expeditions pursued the fugitives along forest trails. One officer even embarked on a raft and chased the Inca far downstream from one jungle encampment to another. He eventually heard that Tupac Amaru was hidden with a tribe of primitive forest Indians many miles downriver from Vilcabamba. This he learned from an Inca general

Inca resistance to Spanish rule, which continued for four decades in the face of seemingly overwhelming odds, is commemorated on the gently rounded sides of this polychrome drinking cup, which shows Inca warriors engaged in dubious battle with Spanish soldiers. Not until 1572, when Viceroy Toledo ordered a "war of fire and blood" to rid himself of "that robbers' den and scarecrow bogey" known as Vilcabamba, last citadel of the Incas, did the long resistance finally collapse.

captured "in a jungle so dense and wild that it would have been impossible to have found him" without the advice of forest tribesmen. The Spaniards captured him by traveling by night, marching through thick jungle lit by torches. Then, in the words of the Spanish officer, "I learned that Tupac Amaru was retreating into the densest part of the Manarí jungle. We traveled into it on foot and unshod, with little food or provisions, for we had lost these on the river." One night, two half-caste soldiers who were leading the search party saw a campfire burning in the distance. Approaching it cautiously, they came upon the Inca Tupac Amaru and his wife warming themselves. The other Spaniards arrived soon after and arrested them.

Tupac Amaru was led back upriver to Vilcabamba and then along the trails to Cuzco. The expedition made a triumphal entry into Cuzco in September 1572 with its captives chained together, the Inca in a cloak and mantle of crimson velvet. A few sacred relics of the Vilcabamba regime were also brought in, among them a golden image of the sun god and the mummified bodies of Manco Inca and Titu Cusi. The last Inca was imprisoned and subjected to an intense campaign of religious indoctrination. Batteries of priests and friars sought to convert Tupac Amaru to Christianity, and eventually he indicated a willingness to convert.

The priests who were instructing the Inca were dismayed to find that Viceroy Toledo intended to execute their charge, his conversion notwithstanding. There was first a summary trial of Tupac Amaru's military commanders, and these warriors were sentenced and hanged for the crime of trying to defend Vilcabamba against the Spaniards. The viceroy's court then turned its attention to the Inca himself, convicting him of responsibility for the deaths of the various Spaniards who had fought in Vilcabamba during the previous decade. This was manifestly unjust, for Tupac Amaru had become Inca only a few months before the invasion that captured him, and many in Cuzco were shocked by the viceroy's determination to execute the last of his line. The city's leading ecclesiastics went down on their knees and begged Viceroy Toledo for mercy, but he was determined for political reasons to remove this final symbol of Inca rule.

Tupac Amaru was led to his execution seated on a black-draped mule. He wore mourning clothes, his hands were tied, and a noose was draped around his neck. So many natives congregated that it was possible to push through the streets and squares of Cuzco only with the greatest difficulty. People were crowded on roofs and walls, and they lined the hills around the city. As the Inca was led down one street by an escort of anti-Inca tribesmen and the viceroy's guard, his sister appeared at a window and cried out to him, "Whither are you going, my brother, prince and sole king of the four *suyus*?" She tried to move toward Tupac Amaru but nearby priests prevented her. Even Spanish ladies were weeping in sympathy for the unfortunate ruler.

When Tupac Amaru reached the scaffold, the great crowd of Indians gathered in the city's central square "deafened the skies, making them reverberate with their cries and wailing." The Inca silenced

them with the familiar gesture of authority, raising his open right hand to his right ear, and then slowly lowering it to his thigh. He then made his remarkable and unexpected speech from the scaffold in which he acknowledged that he had become a Christian and denounced the oracles and religious rituals of his own people. This done, Tupac Amaru was given absolution and his head was placed on the block. The native executioner then bound his eyes, held him on the dais, and, taking Tupac Amaru's hair in his left hand, severed the Inca's head with a single blow of a cutlass and held it high for all to see. At that moment the bells of the cathedral began to toll, followed by those of all the monasteries and parish churches in the city. Almost forty years after the execution of Tupac Amaru's uncle Atahualpa in the central square of Cajamarca, the Conquest of Peru was complete.

With Tupac Amaru's execution, Vilcabamba declined rapidly. The Spaniards tried, for a time, to occupy the remote area, but after a silver mine there was exhausted, the site was abandoned. It was not until the late eighteenth century that interest in this refuge of the Incas revived. The first chapters of this book described expeditions to the ruins of Choquequirau, high above the canyon of the Apurimac, and Hiram Bingham's dramatic discovery, in 1911, of the famous ruins of Machu Picchu. Bingham's team did not stop with this spectacular find but moved on down the Urubamba and up the Vilcabamba River. They investigated another Inca site at a place called Rosapata, and by locating a nearby shrine, Bingham was able to prove that this second discovery was Vitcos—Manco Inca's first capital in the Vilcabamba region, the place where he was almost captured in 1537, and the scene of his murder by fugitives in 1545.

Not content with this success, Bingham pushed northward to follow up another report of a hidden ruin. He and a companion, accompanied by several Indians, walked for days over a pass and down slippery forest trails into the remote Pampaconas valley. There, amid dense Amazonian jungles, Bingham's men cleared the undergrowth from the Inca ruins at a place called Espíritu Pampa. They found a number of buildings, walls, watercourses, and a bridge—all hidden by a dense curtain of vines, creepers, and tall trees. Bingham's attention was captured by a pile of crudely made curved roofing tiles—which, he concluded, indicated the remains of a subsequent Spanish occupation of the Inca site. In 1911 alone Bingham had thus found three Inca ruins of great importance: Machu Picchu, Vitcos, and the mysterious settlement known as Espíritu Pampa, or Plain of the Spirits.

The following year Bingham returned with a larger expedition and cleared and excavated Machu Picchu. A subsequent expedition in 1915 uncovered more Inca ruins on the steep, forested hillsides above the Urubamba. Machu Picchu would be cleared again in the 1930s, and yet another American archaeological expedition, this one in 1940, discovered additional, smaller Inca sites near Machu Picchu. These were part of a chain of terraced villages that lay along the high trail between Machu Picchu and Ollantaytambo. As we have noted, in

Bloody-minded in life and bloodied in death, Francisco Pizarro fell beneath knives wielded by Almagrists in 1541 (right)—assassinated by members of a faction whose leader the Pizarros had put to death three years earlier. In a sense, the Conquest was complete at this point, having claimed all of its principals as victims, but the last chapter was not actually written until three decades later, in 1572, when the forces of Viceroy Toledo captured the last of Peru's Inca monarchs in the Vilcabamba wilderness. Brought to Cuzco in chains, Tupac Amaru was executed (left) as his ill-fated predecessor, Atahualpa, had been, with little regard for justice, mercy, or the importance of his station.

recent years this pathway has been cleared extensively; now known as the Inca Trail, it is one of the world's most beautiful and fascinating hikes.

Hiram Bingham maintained, at first tentatively and then with increasing conviction, that Machu Picchu was in fact the "lost city" of Vilcabamba, the ultimate refuge of Manco Inca and his sons. It was known that ancient Vilcabamba lay two days' march from Vitcos, and Bingham therefore set out, with characteristic determination, to show that he could walk in two days from the rediscovered settlement of Vitcos to Machu Picchu. He advanced various other arguments to support his claim, which was generally accepted for more than fifty years.

It was not until 1964 that Bingham's identification of Machu Picchu as Vilcabamba was seriously contested. The challenger was another American explorer, Gene Savoy, who had retraced Bingham's route down the Pampaconas valley and revisited the jungle ruin of Espíritu Pampa. Savoy probed deeper into the forest around Espíritu Pampa than Bingham had done during his brief visit in 1911, and he thereby discovered a large area of ruins that included some three hundred houses as well as platforms, water channels, and shrines—all buried under layers of forest growth and detritus. Savoy and later visitors also noticed clear evidence of a conflagration in the ruins, and the curious, Spanish-looking roofing tiles.

In my earlier book, *The Conquest of the Incas*, I carefully analyzed all sixteenth-century accounts of Vilcabamba, including some important documents unknown both to Bingham or Savoy, and was able to show that all of the places mentioned in the Spanish chronicles were located on the route from Vitcos to Espíritu Pampa, rather than on the road from Vitcos to Machu Picchu. The newly-discovered description of Vilcabamba as lying in a broad valley rich in tropical produce tallies with Espíritu Pampa—at 2,000 feet above sea level—rather than with Machu Picchu—at an elevation of some 9,000 feet. But the conclusive evidence lies in the roofing tiles, which Bingham and Savoy both remarked upon. Unfortunately, they did not know Martín de Murúa's description of Vilcabamba, in which he noted that Manco's palace was built "on different levels and covered in roof tiles." Here was the proof: a sixteenth-century chronicler had recorded the extraordinary fact that Manco Inca had tried to copy Spanish tiles for his own palace—and no other Inca ruin in the Vilcabamba region or elsewhere in Peru has yielded similar tiles.

Vilcabamba, the final refuge of the Incas, has thus been rediscovered. Ironically, its ruins are too remote and too deeply buried by jungle undergrowth to be worth excavating. Even if twentieth-century archaeologists were to attempt such a feat, there is little likelihood that they would uncover much, for we know from the chronicles that Vilcabamba's citizens burned the city when the Spaniards entered it in June 1572. As a result it will probably remain largely unexplored, a vegetation-choked vestige of the place where Manco Inca tried to re-create the splendors of his ancestors' great empire—and Machu Picchu will remain the enduring symbol of Inca resistance to Spanish tyrany.

MACHU PICCHU
IN LITERATURE

Although he is remembered, first and foremost, as the discoverer of Machu Picchu, Hiram Bingham actually had several careers, as exemplary as they were disparate. The son and grandson of highly regarded missionaries, Bingham was born in Honolulu, received an undergraduate degree from Yale and graduate degrees from the University of California and Harvard, and taught history at both Princeton and his alma mater. During World War I he distinguished himself as an aviator in France, and thereafter he served as Lieutenant Governor, Governor, and Senator from Connecticut. But no event in a lifetime of public service could rival the first. Bingham himself seemed aware of that fact in setting down this account of his 1911 expedition, which opens with a description of the Urubamba River valley and closes with the speculation that Machu Picchu may in fact be Vilcabamba, the last citadel of the Incas.

AN UNBELIEVABLE DREAM

Here the river escapes from the cold plateau by tearing its way through gigantic mountains of granite. The road runs through a land of matchless charm. It has the majestic grandeur of the Canadian Rockies, as well as the startling beauty of the Nuuanu Pali near Honolulu, and the enchanting vistas of the Koolau Ditch Trail on Maui, in my native land. In the variety of its charms and the power of its spell, I know of no place in the world which can compare with it. Not only has it great snow peaks looming above the clouds more than two miles overhead; gigantic precipices of many-colored granite rising sheer for thousands of feet above the foaming, glistening, roaring rapids, it has also, in striking contrast, orchids and tree ferns, the delectable beauty of luxurious vegetation, and the mysterious witchery of the jungle. One is drawn irresistibly onward by ever-recurring surprises through a deep, winding gorge, turning and twisting past overhanging cliffs of incredible height.

Above all, there is the fascination of finding here and there under swaying vines, or perched on top of a beetling crag, the rugged masonry of a bygone race; and of trying to understand the bewildering romance of the ancient builders who, ages ago, sought refuge in a region which appears to have been expressly designed by nature as a sanctuary for the oppressed, a place where they might fearlessly and patiently give expression to their passion for walls of enduring beauty. Space forbids any attempt to describe in detail the constantly changing panorama, the rank tropical foliage, the countless terraces, the towering cliffs, the glaciers peeping out between the clouds. . . .

We passed an ill-kept, grass-thatched hut, turned off the road through a tiny clearing, and made our camp at the edge of the river on a sandy beach. Opposite us, beyond the huge granite bowlders which interfered with the progress of the surging stream, the steep mountain was clothed with thick jungle. Since we were near the road yet protected from the curiosity of passers-by, it seemed to be an ideal spot for a camp. Our actions, however, aroused the suspicions of the owner of the hut, Melchor Arteaga, who leased the lands of Mandor Pampa. He was anxious to know why we did not stay at his "tavern" like other respectable travelers. Fortunately the Prefect of Cuzco, our old friend J. J. Nuñez, had given us an armed escort who spoke Quichua [the Inca tongue]. Our *gendarme*, Sergeant Carrasco, was able to reassure the inn keeper. They had quite a long conversation. When Arteaga learned that we were interested in the architectural remains of the

Incas, and were looking for the palace of the last Inca, he said there were some very good ruins in this vicinity—in fact, some excellent ones on top of the opposite mountain, called Huayna Picchu, and also on a ridge called Machu Picchu!

The morning of July 24th dawned in a cold drizzle. Arteaga shivered and seemed inclined to stay in his hut. I offered to pay him well if he would show me the ruins. He demurred and said it was too hard a climb for such a wet day. But when he found that I was willing to pay him a *sol* (a Peruvian silver dollar, fifty cents, gold), three or four times the ordinary daily wage in this vicinity, he finally agreed to go. When asked just where the ruins were, he pointed straight up to the top of the mountain. No one supposed that they would be particularly interesting. And no one cared to go with me. The Naturalist said there were "more butterflies near the river!" and he was reasonably certain he could collect some new varieties. The Surgeon said he had to wash his clothes and mend them. Anyhow it was my job to investigate all reports of ruins and try to find the Inca capital.

So, accompanied only by Sergeant Carrasco I left camp at ten o'clock. Arteaga took us some distance upstream. On the road we passed a snake which had only just been killed. He said the region was the favorite haunt of "vipers." We later learned the lance-headed or yellow viper, commonly known as the fer-de-lance, a very venomous serpent, capable of making considerable springs when in pursuit of its prey, is common hereabouts.

After a walk of three quarters of an hour Arteaga left the main road and plunged down through the jungle to the bank of the river. Here there was a primitive bridge which crossed the roaring rapids at its narrowest part, where the stream was forced to flow between two great boulders. The "bridge" was made of half a dozen very slender logs, some of which were not long enough to span the distance between the boulders, but had been spliced and lashed together with vines!

Arteaga and the Sergeant took off their shoes and crept gingerly across, using their somewhat prehensile toes to keep from slipping. It was obvious that no one could live for an instant in the icy cold rapids, but would immediately be dashed to pieces against the rocks. I am frank to confess that I got down on my hands and knees and crawled across, six inches at a time. Even after we reached the other side I could not help wondering what would happen to the "bridge" if a particularly heavy shower should fall in the valley above. A light rain had fallen during the night and the river had risen so that the bridge was already threatened by the foaming rapids. It would not take much more to wash it away entirely. If this should happen during the day it might be very awkward. As a matter of fact, it did happen a few days later and when the next visitors attempted to cross the river at this point they found only one slender log remaining.

Leaving the stream, we now struggled up the bank through dense jungle, and in a few minutes reached the bottom of a very precipitous slope. For an hour and twenty minutes we had a hard climb. A good part of the distance we went on all fours, sometimes holding on by our fingernails. Here and there, a primitive ladder made from the roughly notched trunk of a small tree was placed in such a way as to help one over what might otherwise have proved to be an impassable cliff. In another place the slope was covered with slippery grass where it was hard to find either handholds or footholds. Arteaga groaned and said that there were lots of snakes here. Sergeant Carrasco said nothing but was glad he had good military shoes. The humidity was great. We were in the belt of maximum precipitation in Eastern Peru. The heat was excessive; and I was not in training! There were no ruins or *andenes* of any kind in sight. I began to think my companions had chosen the better part.

Shortly after noon, just as we were completely exhausted, we reached a little grass-covered hut 2,000 feet above the river where several good-natured Indians, pleasantly surprised at our unexpected arrival, welcomed us with dripping gourds full of cool, delicious water. Then they set before us a few cooked sweet potatoes. It seems that two Indian farmers, Richarte and Alvarez, had recently chosen this eagles' nest for their home. They said they had found plenty of terraces here on which to grow their crops. Laughingly they admitted they enjoyed being free from undesirable visitors, officials looking for army "volunteers" or collecting taxes.

Richarte told us that they had been living here four years. It seems probable that, owing to its inaccessibility, the canyon had been unoccupied for several centuries, but with the completion of the new government road, settlers began once more to occupy this region. In time somebody clambered up the precipices and found on these slopes at an elevation of 9,000 feet above the sea, an abundance of rich soil conveniently situated on artificial terraces, in a fine climate. Here the Indians had finally cleared off and burned over a few terraces and planted crops of maize, sweet and white potatoes, sugar cane, beans, peppers, tree tomatoes, and gooseberries.

They said there were two paths to the outside world. Of one we had already had a taste; the other was "even more difficult," a perilous path down the face of a rocky precipice on the other side of the ridge. It was their only means of egress in the wet season when the primitive bridge over which we had come could not be maintained. I was not surprised to learn that they went away from home "only about once a month."

Through Sergeant Carrasco I learned that the ruins were "a little further along." In this country one never can tell whether such a report is worthy of credence. "He may have been lying" is a good footnote to affix to all hearsay evidence. Accordingly, I was not unduly excited, nor in a great hurry to move. The heat was still great, the water from the Indians' spring was cool and delicious, and the rustic wooden bench, hospitably covered immediately after my arrival with a soft woolen poncho, seemed most comfortable. Furthermore, the view was simply enchanting. Tremendous green precipices fell away to the white rapids of the Urubamba below. Immediately in front, on the north side of the valley, was a great granite cliff rising 2,000 feet sheer. To the left was the solitary peak of Huayna Picchu, surrounded by seemingly inaccessible precipices. On all sides were rocky cliffs. Beyond them cloud-capped snow-covered mountains rose thousands of feet above us.

140

We continued to enjoy the wonderful view of the canyon, but all the ruins we could see from our cool shelter were a few terraces.

Without the slightest expectation of finding anything more interesting than the ruins of two or three stone houses such as we had encountered at various places on the road between Ollantaytambo and Torontoy, I finally left the cool shade of the pleasant little hut and climbed farther up the ridge and around a slight promontory. Melchor Arteaga had "been there once before," so he decided to rest and gossip with Richarte and Alvarez. They sent a small boy with me as a "guide." The Sergeant was in duty bound to follow, but I think he may have been a little curious to see what there was to see.

Hardly had we left the hut and rounded the promontory than we were confronted with an unexpected sight, a great flight of beautifully constructed stone-faced terraces, perhaps a hundred of them, each hundreds of feet long and ten feet high. They had been recently rescued from the jungle by the Indians. A veritable forest of large trees which had been growing on them for centuries had been chopped down and partly burned to make a clearing for agricultural purposes. The task was too great for the two Indians so the tree trunks had been allowed to lie as they fell and only the smaller branches removed. But the ancient soil, carefully put in place by the Incas, was still capable of producing rich crops of maize and potatoes.

However, there was nothing to be excited about. Similar flights of well-made terraces are to be seen in the upper Urubamba Valley at Pisac and Ollantaytambo, as well as opposite Torontoy. So we patiently followed the little guide along one of the widest terraces where there had once been a small conduit and made our way into an untouched forest beyond. Suddenly I found myself confronted with the walls of ruined houses built of the finest quality of Inca stone work. It was hard to see them for they were partly covered with trees and moss, the growth of centuries, but in the dense shadow, hiding in bamboo thickets and tangled vines, appeared here and there walls of white granite ashlars carefully cut and exquisitely fitted together. We scrambled along through the dense undergrowth, climbing over terrace walls and in bamboo thickets where our guide found it easier going than I did. Suddenly without any warning, under a huge overhanging ledge the boy showed me a cave beautifully lined with the finest cut stone. It had evidently been a Royal Mausoleum. On top of this particular ledge was a semi-circular building whose outer wall, gently sloping and slightly curved bore a striking resemblance to the famous Temple of the Sun in Cuzco. This might also be a Temple of the Sun. It followed the natural curvature of the rock and was keyed to it by one of the finest examples of masonry I had ever seen. Furthermore it was tied into another beautiful wall, made of very carefully matched ashlars of pure white granite, especially selected for its fine grain. Clearly, it was the work of a master artist. The interior surface of the wall was broken by niches and square stone-pegs. The exterior surface was perfectly simple and unadorned. The lower courses, of particularly large ashlars, gave it a look of solidity. The upper courses, diminishing in size toward the top, lent grace and delicacy to the structure. The flowing lines, the symmetrical arrangement of the ashlars, and the gradual gradation of the courses, combined to produce a wonderful effect, softer and more pleasing than that of the marble temples of the Old World. Owing to the absence of mortar, there were no ugly spaces between the rocks. They might have grown together. On account of the beauty of the white granite this structure surpassed in attractiveness the best Inca walls in Cuzco which had caused visitors to marvel for four centuries. It seemed like an unbelievable dream. Dimly, I began to realize that this wall and its adjoining semicircular temple over the cave were as fine as the finest stonework in the world.

It fairly took my breath away. What could this place be? Why had no one given us any idea of it? Even Melchor Arteaga was only moderately interested and had no appreciation of the importance of the ruins which Richarte and Alvarez had adopted for their little farm. Perhaps after all this was an isolated small place which had escaped notice because it was inaccessible.

Then the little boy urged us to climb up a steep hill over what seemed to be a flight of stone steps. Surprise followed surprise in bewildering succession. We came to a great stairway of large granite blocks. Then we walked along a path to a clearing where the Indians had planted a small vegetable garden. Suddenly we found ourselves standing in front of the ruins of two of the finest and most interesting structures in ancient America. Made of beautiful white granite, the walls contained blocks of Cyclopean size, higher than a man. The sight held me spellbound.

Each building had only three walls and was entirely open on one side. The principal temple had walls twelve feet high which were lined with exquisitely made niches, five, high up at each end, and seven on the back. There were seven courses of ashlars in the end walls. Under the seven rear niches was a rectangular block fourteen feet long, possibly a sacrificial altar, but more probably a throne for the mummies of departed Incas, brought out to be worshipped. The building did not look as though it ever had a roof. The top course of beautifully smooth ashlars was not intended to be covered, so the sun could be welcomed here by priests and mummies. I could scarcely believe my senses as I examined the larger blocks in the lower course and estimated that they must weigh from ten to fifteen tons each. Would anyone believe what I had found? Fortunately, in this land where accuracy in reporting what one has seen is not a prevailing characteristic of travelers, I had a good camera and the sun was shining.

The principal temple faces the south where there is a small plaza or courtyard. On the east side of the plaza was another amazing structure, the ruins of a temple containing three great windows looking out over the canyon to the rising sun. Like its neighbor, it is unique among Inca ruins. Nothing just like them in design and execution has ever been found. Its three conspicuously large windows, obviously too large to serve any useful purpose, were most beautifully made with the greatest care and solidity. This was clearly a ceremonial edifice of peculiar significance. Nowhere else in Peru, so far as I know, is there a similar structure conspicuous for being "a masonry wall with three windows." It will be remembered that Salcamayhua, the Peruvian who wrote an account of the antiquities of Peru in 1620 said that the first Inca, Manco the Great, ordered "works to be executed at the place of his birth, consisting of a masonry wall with three windows." Was that what I had found? If it was, then this was not the capital of the last Inca but the birthplace of the first. It did not occur to me that it might be both. To be sure the region was one which could fit in with the requirements of Tampu Tocco, the place of refuge of the civilized folk who fled from the southern barbarian tribes after the battle of La Raya and brought with them the body of their king Pachacutec who was slain by an arrow. He might have been buried in the stone-lined cave under the semi-circular temple.

Could this be "the principal city" of Manco and his sons, that Vilcapampa where was the "University of Idolatry" which Friar Marcos and Friar Diego had tried to reach. It behooved us to find out as much about it as we could.

HIRAM BINGHAM
Lost City of the Incas, 1948

A PLACE CALLED TAMPU-TOCCO

By 1930, when he wrote Machu Picchu, A Citadel of the Incas, *Hiram Bingham had seriously inflated his claims for the enigmatic ruins he had found. No longer content to speculate on their origin and significance, he averred that there was "no question" in his mind that the ruins he had happened upon in the summer of 1911 were those of the mythic city of Tampu-tocco, birthplace of the first Inca.*

The more one studies the beautiful masonry of the citadel of Machu Picchu, the more one marvels that a people so skilful should have been willing to spend so much time and labor in such a remote inhospitable corner of the Andes; and the more one wishes that the builders had practiced the art of writing and had left behind them decipherable inscriptions which in the course of time might have been translated to tell us something of their history. The story of Mesopotamia, Egypt, and the classic lands of the Mediterranean was fortunately confided to clay tablets, stone inscriptions, and manuscripts of papyrus and vellum, but except for the remarkable hieroglyphic date stones of the Mayas the story of the prehistoric America has no such kindly aids for those who would investigate it. Its historians must piece together contradictory traditions, fragments of cloth and pottery, ruins of houses, temples, and terraces, and such artifacts as can be obtained, and from these put together what must be at best a very fragmentary story on the details of which no two experts probably ever will agree. The best that one can do is patiently to study all the evidence which can be collected, and put together a story which at least is not capable of being destroyed by any known incontrovertible evidence. Since the stories which have come down to us from the early *conquistadores* and their descendants, like Garcilasso Inca de la Vega, are so contradictory and conflicting, their evidence can hardly ever be said to be incontrovertible. Where it runs clearly counter to the known habits of the highlanders and the evidence gained by excavation and observation it may be accepted as less likely to be true than statements not so substantiated.

The popular picture of the civilization of the Incas is based on Prescott's charming account, which in turn was based largely on the writings of Garcilasso, himself the son of an Inca princess. Unfortunately for the accuracy of Garcilasso, however, he left Peru when a boy in his teens, never returned, lived most of his life in Spain, and did not write his celebrated chronicles of the Incas until he was an old man. In the intervening years he had presumably repeated frequently the stories of the land of his birth and his mother's people. He knew what pleased and astonished his European auditors, he knew what shocked them, he knew what seemed to them reasonable and admirable, altogether worthy of praise. It was natural, therefore, that in the course of the thirty or forty years of his life in Spain before he began to write his book he should have come to believe that his mother's people were quite different from what they really were. He wanted Europeans to admire his maternal ancestors and he wrote his book accordingly, his boyish recollections being colored, perhaps consciously, perhaps to a large degree unconsciously, by the requirements of his audience.

A writer who has recently begun to come into his own, Fernando Montesinos, an ecclesiastical lawyer of the seventeenth century, wrote a different sort of book. He appears to have gone to Peru in 1629 as the follower of that well-known viceroy, the Count of Chinchon, whose wife was cured of malaria by the use of Peruvian bark or quinine and was instrumental in the introduction of this medicine into Europe— a fact that has been commemorated in the botanical name of the genus *Cinchona*. Montestinos was well educated and appears to have given himself over entirely to historical research. He traveled extensively in Peru and wrote several books. His history of the Incas was spoiled by the introduction, in which, as might have been expected of an orthodox ecclesiastical lawyer, he contended that Peru was peopled under the leadership of Ophir, the great grandson of Noah. Pushing aside his clerical prejudices, however, one finds his work to be of great value, and the late Sir Clements Markham, foremost of English students of Peruvian archaeology, was inclined to place considerable credence in the statements of Montesinos.

In Montesinos there are a number of references to a place called Tampu-tocco, from which the Spaniards were apparently told that the Incas came. "Tampu" means "a place of temporary abode or a tavern"; "tocco" means "window." "Tampu" may also mean "an improved piece of ground or farm far from the town."

... Montesinos states that after the death in battle of Pachacuti VI, last of the great Amautas or kings who ruled Peru for more than sixty generations, the remains of his faithful followers retired to the mountains, going to Tampu-tocco, which was a healthy place where they hid the body of their king in a cave and where they were found by refugees fleeing from the general chaos and disorder which followed the invasion of the southern barbarians. Montesinos says they made their capital at Tampu-tocco and elected a king, Titi Truaman Quicho. Under him and his successors the people of Tampu-tocco lived for over five hundred years, all record of which is lost.

Clearly Tampu-tocco must have been a place remote, well defended by nature from the rest of the Peruvian plateau, or it would not have been possible for the disorganized remnant of Pachacuti VI's army

to have taken refuge there and set up an independent kingdom with only five hundred armed followers. The Spainards who asked about Tampu-tocco got the impression that it was at or near Paccari-tampu, a small town eight or ten miles south of Cuzco, in the vicinity of which there are the ruins of a small Inca town and near it a little hill consisting of several large rocks the surface of which is carved into platforms and in one place into two sleeping pumas, and beneath which are caves said to have been used recently by political refugees. There is enough about the characteristics of the remains near Paccari-tampu to lend color to the story frequently told to the early Spaniards that this was Tampu-tocco. Yet the surrounding region is not difficult. There are no precipices. There are no natural defenses against the invading force which captured the neighboring valley of Cuzco. A few men might have hid in the caves of Paccari-tampu but it was no place where an independent kingdom might readily have been established by a disorganized handful of the followers and chief priests of Pachacuti VI. Furthermore, there are no windows in the architecture which would justify the name of Tampu-tocco—a place of temporary abode or farm far from a town, and characterized by windows.

The citadel of Machu Picchu, on the other hand, is such a place.

We know that Cuzco was practically deserted. Apparently it was sacked by the invaders. The chief remnants of the members of the old *régime* enjoyed living at Tampu-tocco, says Montesinos, because there is the very famous cave where the Incas, as the historians say, first originated and where, they firmly assert, there never have existed such things as earthquakes, plagues, or tremblings; and because, if fortune should turn against their new young king and he should be killed, they could bury him and hide him in this cave as in a very sacred place. Apparently, then, this was the place where they hid the body of Pachacuti VI, probably in the cave under the Semicircular Temple at Machu Picchu. At any rate, fortune was kind to the founders of Tampu-tocco. They had chosen an excellent place of refuge where they were not disturbed and their ruler became known as the king of Tampu-tocco, but to him and his successors nothing worth recording happened for many centuries until the establishment of the kingdom in Cuzco. During a period roughly estimated at five hundred years, but which may have been longer or shorter, several of the kings of Tampu-tocco wished to establish themselves in Cuzco, where the great Amautas had reigned for so many centuries, but they were obliged to give up the plan for one reason or another until a king called Tupac Cauri, who had chosen also to call himself Pachacuti VII, began to regain the power of his ancestors and reconquer some of the cities and provinces adjacent to Tampu-tocco. Montesinos says he attempted to abolish idolatry and other evil practices which had become widespread since the overthrow of the old *régime*. He sent messengers to various parts of the highlands asking the people to stop worshiping idols and animals, to cease practicing evil customs which had grown up since the fall of the Amautas, and to return to the ways of their ancestors, but he met with little encouragement. His ambassadors were killed and very little reform took place.

Tupac Cauri, discouraged by the failure of his attempts at reformation and desirous of learning its cause, was told by his soothsayers that the matter which most displeased the gods was the use of letters. Thereupon he ordered that under penalty of death nobody should use the kind of letters with which they had begun to write upon parchment and the leaves of certain trees. This mandate was observed with such strictness that the Peruvians never again used letters until the coming of the Spaniards. Instead, they used threads, strings, and knots, the simple mnemonic device called the *quipu*.

The above is a very curious and interesting tradition relating to an event supposed to have occurred many centuries before the Spanish Conquest. We have no ocular evidence to support it. The skeptic may brush it aside as a story intended to appeal to the vanity of persons with Inca blood in their veins, yet it is not told by the half-caste Garcilasso, but by that careful investigator, Montesinos, a pure-blooded Spaniard. As a matter of fact, to students of Professor Sumner's "mores" and "folkways" the story rings true. Some young fellow, brighter than the rest, had developed a system of ideographs which he scratched on broad smooth leaves. It worked. People were beginning to adopt it. The conservative priests, however, did not like it: there was danger lest some of the precious secrets heretofore handed down orally from priest to neophyte might become public property. Nevertheless, the invention was so useful that it began to spread rapidly. There followed some extremely unlucky event—perhaps an epidemic, or at all events something regarded as extremely unfortunate from the point of view of the ruler. What more natural than that the newly discovered ideograph should be blamed for it? As a result the king, aided and abetted by the priests, determined to abolish this new thing. Its usefulness had not yet been firmly established; in fact, it was inconvenient. The leaves blew away or withered, dried, and cracked, and the writings were lost. Had the idea been permitted to exist a little longer someone would have found how easy it was to scratch ideographs on rocks, and then it would have persisted. The rulers and priests, however, found that the records of tribute to be paid, for instance, could perfectly well be kept by means of the *quipus*, with the additional advantage that the importance of those whose duty it was to remember what each string stood for was assured. The plague passed away, everyone breathed easier, and no one realized at the time how near the Peruvians had come to developing a written language. After all, there is nothing strange or unlikely about such a supposition. One has only to look at the history of Spain itself to realize that royal bigotry and priestly intolerance crushed any new ideas that were arising in that country during the reign of Philip II, and the banishment of hard-working, artistic Moors and clever, businesslike Jews made it impossible for Spain to take that place in modern European history to which the discoveries of her navigators and the courage of her soldiers entitled her.

Since the account in Montesinos relates to an event centuries old at the time of his investigations, it is barely possible that the old method of writing which is referred to in the tradition is the use of record stones and incised terra-cotta cubes, such as have been found in large numbers in the oldest part of Machu Picchu. Stone counters, "poker chips," "dice," and other tokens of a sort not used by the Incas undoubtedly represent an ancient method of counting. In the more recently built parts of Machu Picchu practically none of the record stones were found, nor were there any in the graves which contained the more recent skeletal material together with the typical Inca pottery of "Cuzco style." Obviously, the last inhabitants of the citadel did not use the record stone when they were there. The invention of the far more convenient *quipu* had caused the use of uncertain, easily displaced stone counters to disappear.

Montesinos, continuing his description of the kingdom of Tampu-tocco, takes it for granted that Tampu-tocco was at Paccari-tampu, as all the other chroniclers have done even though there is so little there which fits into the requirements of the case. He says that Tupac Cauri established in Tampu-tocco a kind of university where boys were taught the use of *quipus*, the method of counting, and the significance of the different colored strings, while their fathers and older brothers were trained in military exercises—in other words, practiced with the sling, the bolas, and the war-club, perhaps also with bows and arrows. Thus around the name of Tupac Cauri, Pachacuti VII, the story of various things which took place during the Dark Ages in Tampu-tocco is gathered. Finally, there came the end of this epoch when the royalty and the military efficiency of the little kingdom were on a high plane. The ruler and his counselors, ever bearing in mind the tradition of their ancestors who centuries before had dwelt in Cuzco, determined to make the attempt to reëstablish themselves there. Their effort failed. An earthquake which ruined many buildings in Cuzco, caused rivers to change their courses, destroyed many towns, and was followed by the outbreak of a disastrous epidemic, determined them to give up their plans. In Tampu-tocco there was no pestilence; apparently the earthquake did not affect that point. It is worth recalling to mind in this connection that a severe earthquake in Cuzco would do great damage at Paccari-tampu, less than ten miles away. It might, however, do none at Machu Picchu, located, as it is, in the heart of an intrusive granite formation where, so far as one can judge from the condition of the ancient buildings, there have been no very severe earthquakes.

In the following years the inhabitants of Tampu-tocco became more and more crowded. Every available square yard of arable land had been terraced and cultivated. The men were intelligent, well organized, and accustomed to discipline, but they could not raise enough food for their families; so at length they set out to find arable land, under the leadership of the active, energetic ruler of the day, whose name was Manco Ccapac.

There are many stories of the rise of Manco Ccapac, who, when he had grown to man's estate, assembled his people to see how he could secure new lands for them. After consultation with his brothers, he determined to set out with them "toward the hill over which the sun rose," as we are informed by Pachacutiyamqui Salcamayhua, an Indian who was a descendant of a long line of Incas, whose great-grandparents lived in the time of the Spanish Conquest, and who wrote an account of the antiquities of Peru in 1620. He gives the history of the Incas as it was handed down to the descendants of the former rulers of Peru. In it we read that Manco Ccapac and his brothers succeeded in reaching Cuzco and settled there. Manco married one of his own sisters in order that he might not lose caste and that no other family be elevated by this marriage to an equality with his. He made good laws, conquered many provinces, and is regarded as the founder of the Inca dynasty properly so-called. The Ttahuantinsuyus, ancient name for the highlanders of Peru, soon came under his sway with good grace and brought him rich presents. The Inca, as Manco Ccapac now came to be called, was recognized as the most powerful chief, the most valiant fighter, and the most lucky warrior in the Andes. His captains and soldiers were brave, well disciplined, and well armed. All his affairs prospered greatly. "Afterward he ordered works to be executed at the place of his birth, consisting of a masonry wall with three windows, which were emblems of the house of his fathers whence he descended." The windows were named for his paternal and maternal grandparents and his uncles.

So far as is known at present, there is no place in Peru, except at Machu Picchu, where the ruins consist of anything like a "masonry wall with three windows" of such a ceremonial character as is here referred to. There is no question in my mind, therefore, that the Temple of the Three Windows, which has been described as the most interesting structure within the citadel, is the building mentioned in the chronicle written by Pachacutiyamqui Salcamayhua in 1620.

Although none of the other ancient chronicles give the story of the first Inca ordering a memorial wall to be built at the place of his birth, they nearly all tell of his having come from a place called Tampu-tocco, or a country place remarkable for its windows. To be sure, the only place assigned by them as the location of Tampu-tocco is Paccari-tampu, which, as has been said, is about eight or ten miles southwest of Cuzco and has some interesting ruins; but careful examination shows that there were no windows in the buildings of Paccari-tampu and nothing to justify its having such a name as Tampu-tocco. The climate of Paccari-tampu, like that of most places in the highlands, is too severe to invite or encourage the use of windows, while to high-landers accustomed to the climatic conditions of Cuzco and vicinity the climate of Machu Picchu must have seemed mild and consequently the use of windows was agreeable. As a result, the buildings of Machu Picchu have far more windows than any other important ruin in Peru.

Nevertheless we should have more difficulty in abandoning the testimony of a majority of the chroniclers in favor of Tampu-tocco and Paccari-tampu were it not for the existing contemporary records of a legal inquiry made by the viceroy Francisco de Toledo in 1572 at the time when he put to death Tupac Amaru, the last Inca. On the twenty-first of January, 1572, fifteen Indians who were descended from those who used to live near the important salt terraces around Cuzco, on being questioned, agreed that they had heard their fathers and grandfathers repeat the tradition that the first Inca, Manco Ccapac, came from Tampu-tocco when he arrived to take their lands away from their ancestors. They did not say that the first Inca came from Paccari-tampu, which, it seems to me, would have been a most natural thing for them to have said if it were true. In addition to this testimony, there is the still older testimony of some Indians born before the arrival of Pizarro, who, two years before, in 1570, were examined at a legal investigation made at Xauxa. The oldest witness, ninety-five years of age, on being sworn, said that Manco Ccapac was lord of the town where he was born and had conquered Cuzco but that he had never heard what town it was that Manco came from. The Indian chief who followed him was ninety-four years old and also denied that he knew where Manco Ccapac was born. Another chief, aged ninety-two, testified that Manco Ccapac came out of a cave called Tocco and that he was lord of the town near that cave. Not one of the witnesses stated that Manco Ccapac came from Paccari-tampu, although it is difficult to imagine why they should not have done so if, as the Spaniards believe, this was the original Tampu-tocco. At all events, there is an interesting cave at Paccari-tampu and the chroniclers, not one of whom knew of the important ruins at Machu Picchu, were willing enough to assume that this was the place where the first Inca was born and from which he came to conquer Cuzco. Yet it seems hardly possible that the old Indians should have forgotten entirely where Tampu-tocco was. Their reticence in regard to it must be laid, it seems to me, to the fact of its having been so successfully kept secret by reason of its location in a remote place whither the followers of Pachacuti VI fled with his body after the overthrow of the old *régime*, and in the same remote fastness of the Andes to which the young Inca Manco fled from Cuzco in the days of Pizarro.

Certainly the requirements of Tampu-tocco described in Montesinos are met at Machu Picchu. The splendid natural defenses of the Grand Canyon of the Urubamba made it an ideal refuge for the descendants of the Amautas during the five or six hundred years of lawlessness and confusion which succeeded the barbarian invasions from the plains to the east and south. The scarcity of violent earthquakes, and also the healthfulness, both marked characteristics of Tampu-tocco, are met at Machu Picchu. The evidence of both pottery and record stones points to an era preceding Inca times. The story of Pachacutiyamqui Salcamayhua of the construction of a memorial wall with three windows at the place of Manco Ccapac's birth points clearly to Machu Picchu. Machu Picchu also meets the requirements of a place whose existence might easily have been concealed by those who were in the secret, and whose location might have been unknown to a large part of the population at the time of the Spanish Conquest.

Accordingly, I am convinced that the name of the older part of Machu Picchu was Tampu-tocco, that here Pachacuti VI was buried, and that here was the capital of the little kingdom where, during the centuries—possibly eight or ten—between the Amautas and the Incas, there were kept alive the wisdom, skill, and best traditions of the ancient folk who had developed the civilization of Peru, using agricultural terraces as its base. It seems to me quite probable that Manco Ccapac, after he had established himself as Inca in Cuzco, should have built a fine temple to the honor of his ancestors. Ancestor worship was common among the Incas and nothing would have been more reasonable than the construction of the Temple of the Three Windows in their honor.

HIRAM BINGHAM
Machu Picchu: A Citadel of the Incas, 1930

149

Like Hiram Bingham, Gene Savoy was an avid amateur archaeologist and an autodidact who might have been speaking for his illustrious predecessor when he wrote, in the introduction to *Antisuyo: The Search for the Lost Cities of the Amazon,* "Men dream of adventure and I am no exception. I cannot remember not wanting to be an explorer." Like Bingham, Savoy was a student of the chronicles of the Conquest, sixteenty-century journals that attested to the existence and recorded the eventual eradication of Vilcabamba, the legendary last citadel of the Incas. And like Bingham, Savoy combined a careful reading of the chronicles with intuition and audacity in the field. This combination of attributes brought Bingham to the gates of Machu Picchu in 1911; half a century later it was to bring Savoy to the gates of Vilcabamba itself.

The story of Vilcabamba (Willkapampa, in the Quechua language) is a puzzle because so little is known about it. The name Willka was the old name for the sun. It also denotes lineage, descent, ancestry. There is a narcotic plant of the same name, used by the Inca priests to make contact with the spirits of the dead. The name has always held a special place among the Incas. Pampa means plain. Willkapampa was a name that meant the Plain of the Sun and had something to do with the ancestry of the Incas. Fernando Montesinos, secretary to the Spanish Viceroy and chronicler of Inca legend and myth, wrote that in the early days of Peru's history—many centuries before the Spanish takeover—the fifty-third king or *amauta* of prehistoric Peru had successfully defended the Inca empire against an invasion of barbarian tribes coming up from the plains of Argentina, Bolivia and the Titicaca region. Following the defeat of these aliens from the east, the Inca was given the name of Willkanota or Vilcanota. Later, during the reign of his son Pachacuti, a barbarian host again attacked the Incas killing the king in battle and forcing his armies to retreat back to the "place of their origin," Tamputocco, a territory that mythology says was in the Urubamba-Apurímac basins.

The vast Inca empire was known as Tahuantinsuyo, or the land of four parts.... Much larger than modern Peru, the empire included parts of Ecuador, Bolivia, Argentina and Chile and its influence was probably felt into Brazil, Colombia and Venezuela. Cuntisuyo, the temperate region of the Cuzco area, was the land of the Quechua or Cuntis people. Kollasuyo included the high country of Bolivia, Chile and Argentina and was inhabited by the Kollas or Aymaras. Chinchaysuyo, the desert regions occupied by the Chinchas or Yungas, stretched clear up to Quito, Ecuador. The most interesting quarter, and the least known, was Antisuyo (for which the Andes Mountains are named). This was the world beyond the snowy mountains, that great jungle land of the Antis people, sometimes called Yungas, which was the largest quarter geographically, and presumably densely populated. Legend tells (we are not certain just when this event was supposed to have taken place in Inca history) that Cuzco was overthrown by invading people from the eastern forests on the Bolivian side and the Incas were driven out. The story goes on to say that the empire was later solidified again. We do know that during the rule of Huayna Capac in the late fifteenth and early sixteenth centuries of our era, these forest tribes ... continued to attack, posing a constant threat to the Inca capital....

According to the oral traditions of the Incas, after the defeat of the early, unrecorded Inca dynasty (which I assume preceded the first known ruler of the Incas, Manco Capac, who established his capital at Cuzco sometime in the eleventh century A.D.), the whole empire collapsed and small kingdoms were forced out of the provinces. Folklore says the Incas were exiled for six centuries, a period of earthquakes and pestilence. When the exile ended, Manco Capac came up from his refuge at Tamputocco and returned to Cuzco and built a new dynasty of Inca kings who, according to the story, began to retake the old provinces, reuniting the people and establishing a sovereign rule up to the time of the Spanish Conquest. They were penetrating into the populous Amazon forests when the war between Huáscar and Atahualpa paralized the empire. With the triumph of Atahualpa, a conquering-type Inca with his eyes focused on greater expansion, the Incas were ready to begin again; but Pizarro put a stop to it. Perhaps the industrious Inca conqueror would have gone on to invade the eastern forests and the Chibcha, Maya and Aztec empires to the north. Spanish sailors reported having observed Inca sea vessels plying the coast as far as Panama and there is some evidence that they were aware of the existence of the Atlantic Ocean. The Amazon River may have been the route taken, for the Spaniards also reported having seen settlements of the interior spread along the banks of the Amazon.

Had Manco II, descendant of the mighty Manco I (Manco Capac) who had originally led his people out of Tamputocco to found the city of Cuzco, imagined himself the leader of a new sacred cause? Was his cry, "back to the place of origin from whence we will rebuild and reconquer"? He may have believed history was being repeated. This is suggested by the religious fervor of his earlier movement. He took pains to remove the golden mummies of his ancestors and took along a large delegation of priests and Virgins of the Sun by which to preserve the solar arts and sciences of Inca civilization. He also retired with the *coya* and the royal harem to provide for his inheritance.

Was this land of Vilcabamba the Tamputocco of Inca legend, the cave of origin? Hiram Bingham, the Yale University professor, started looking for the "Lost City of the Incas" and chanced upon Machu Picchu northwest of Cuzco. He believed this mountain citadel to be Tamputocco as well as Manco's Vilcabamba—a hypothesis that has been criticized by scholars. As far as I could tell from my study of Inca mythology, there were three caves of origin, the most prominent being at Pacaricctampu in the province of Paruru, south of Cuzco. At least four great nomadic tribes were involved over different periods, the earliest of which seems to have originated in the Apurímac-Urubamba watershed.

While I felt that the region between the Apurímac and Urubamba, *i.e.,* the Vitcos-Vilcabamba territory, was more than likely one of the earliest homes of the Incas before their march on Cuzco, it was also probable that greater Antisuyo—that vast region east of the Andes—was the ancient home of many families that grew into the Inca people. If this were true, then the farther east I explored, the more primitive the constructions that would be found. Because Machu Picchu—and other ancient remains found in and around Cuzco—are the result of

151

a classic period of Inca civilization, the stonework being most technical and the result of advanced skills, it had to be ruled out as both an early home and refuge of the Incas.

Spanish chronicles had placed the central city of Manco in that vigorous land between the Apurímac and Urubamba, deep down in the steaming jungles forty to sixty leagues (six to eight days' foot travel) northwest of Cuzco. . . . On this assumption—and the records of reliable writers—I believed that I could expect to find the missing city in that vicinity. If I succeeded in finding it in the jungles it would lend strength to the idea that ancient peoples, Incas included, were no strangers to the jungle. . . .

Sunday, July 12. On the Trail to Espíritu Pampa

Our little caravan sets out again, moving slowly over the fern-covered trail. The lead men have a hard time cutting a swath wide enough for the pack animals. Winding our way along the path—which looks as if it may have been an old Inca road centuries ago—we come to a promontory that overlooks the lower Concevidayoc Valley spread out directly below, a forested pampa guarded by a 6,600-foot peak and graced by cascading waterfalls. A tiny toy-like farmhouse and a dozen acres of land stand on the edge of the dense virgin rain forest. A series of forested pampas are fed by several rivers that have their origin in the high, rocky Markacocha-Pichqacocha range, a 12,500-foot series of granite peaks some fifty to twenty miles to the west. . . .

A fertile valley irrigated naturally by rivers, the pampas of Espíritu Pampa could have supported a large population. History does not tell us how many people Manco took with him but we can estimate that there were thousands; sources place the figure at anywhere from 30,000 to 100,000. Just how many he maintained at the principal city we do not know. Titu Cusi must have kept his army in the capital city and since it was the metropolis of the province, it can be assumed that constant water supply would have been a chief requirement for the livelihood of a large population. Small mountain citadels like Machu Picchu could neither accommodate nor sustain the agricultural needs of large numbers of people.

Located at the crossroads, Espíritu Pampa affords access to the sierra by means of the road over which we had come. No doubt there were other roads that led up over the Markacocha-Pichqacocha range and down to the Apurímac where an old Inca bridge spans the river. Manco crossed this stream on numerous occasions to attack the Spanish supply lines operating between Huamanga or Ayacucho and Lima, with surprising success. Navigable waters were only two days down river; thus making the highways of the inner jungles accessible to the Incas. . . .

We scramble up a wooded incline and find ourselves on an elevated platform. Benjamin motions for me to follow. He chops his way along a stone wall and drops down into a depression. I wiggle my way through an opening and nearly bump my head on the upper half of a large Inca aryballoid water jar, perched atop a fallen tree. I straighten up and, looking around, see that we are standing inside an ancient Inca room. We set to work clearing the ruins, pulling vines off the walls exposing niches and a doorway at one side. . . . I had crawled through

LEGEND TURNED INTO HISTORY

without knowing what it was. My attention is drawn to the large number of ceramic fragments scattered about the floor. Benjamin tells me there are many such pieces. Minutes later we press into a second, adjacent room. Atop the platform are a series of galleries so overgrown with vegetation I cannot estimate their size or importance. (When I had the buildings cleared, a task that took three precious days out of our schedule, the two-story platform group was found to consist of twelve rooms graced with niches and doorways, including a semicircular room, inner and outer courtyards, a fountain, hallway and stairways, the whole surrounded by high walls decorated with roof pegs. The terraced complex measured 165 by 105 feet.) I notice an unusual piece of orange-red ceramic protruding from the ground. I pick it up and discover that it is roofing tile, the kind used by the Spaniards during colonial times. Kicking up a pile of dead leaves with the heel of my boot, I find there are several layers of tile strewn about the floor. Many pieces are well preserved, colors still vivid. One piece is incised with serpentine lines, an Inca characteristic. The men scratch around the soft floor of the jungle with their machetes and expose piles of similar *teja* mixed with pottery fragments.... Who had used these tiles? Unknown in old Peru, roofing tile was introduced by the Spaniards shortly following the conquest. The Incas preferred ichu straw. Then I remembered that Manco had taken Spanish prisoners of war. These and the Augustinian friars under Titu Cusi may have passed on the use of this permanent roofing material. The Incas would have been adept at making such tiles; they had worked clay for centuries. The Viceroy had ordered the city of Cuzco tiled in the year 1560, a preventative against fire (Manco had put the old capital to the torch in 1536). From our findings it would appear that the Incas of Vilcabamba learned the art of manufacturing roofing tile and were utilizing it in their modern buildings; proof that they were experiencing a kind of transition, absorbing Spanish refinements while retaining their own....

Turning back over our trail we find a long Inca building, its walls fallen, covered by a carpet of dense vegetation. I cannot estimate its dimensions. It is built of rough-hewn stones cemented with mud. Our guide explains this was the extent of the ruins of Eromboni as shown him by the Machiguengas. This compared to what Bingham had described in his book on Machu Picchu. Upon my return to Lima I reviewed his volume *Along the Unchartered Pampaconas*, also his plan of Eromboni Pampa, our Spanish Palace, and found he had observed the roofing tile, "... half a dozen crude Spanish roofing tiles, baked red. All the pieces and fragments we could find would not have covered four square feet. They were of widely different sizes, as though someone had been experimenting. Perhaps an Inca who had seen the new tile roofs of Cuzco had tried to reproduce them here in the jungle, but without success." While he dismissed this find as vague and unimportant, I seized upon it at once. To me it was a key find. Bingham had also been shown the long structure. He gave its measurements as 192 feet long by 24 feet wide and guessed it originally contained twenty-four doors. It seemed odd to me that this was the extent of the ruins of Espíritu Pampa or Eromboni Pampa. Why hadn't the Machiguengas encountered more? Later I learned that their old hunting trail to the higher ground intersects the two major groups of ruins encountered by Bingham—and our own expedition. A practical people, not being curious about anything outside their primitive world of reality, any ruins which they might encounter are cast off as natural stones. Having no concept of numbers or size, they are not able to recognize the significance of antiquities. These reasons, plus their superstition regarding the pampa, explain why they confessed ignorance of other ruins upon Bingham's careful questioning through Saavedra. This prompted Bingham to bring his explorations of the area to a close.

It is with a sigh of relief that we come out into the open air and sunlight some minutes later, away from the steaming forest. A refreshing breeze blows over the valley. We saunter over to Benjamin's cabaña, a quarter of an hour's walk from the main house. Learning of our interest in antiquities—I had mentioned the pottery I had seen at Pucyura—Benjamin informs us that he and the other men of the family have come upon similar objects during their farming. He produces three Inca ceramic pieces and a fourth which appears to be of Tiahuanaco style. Other assorted pieces are displayed, including a blue stone carved in the shape of a tooth, a copper rod, and an old-fashioned Spanish-type horseshoe—a large, flat type used in colonial days. The object had been uncovered while erecting the main house. This isolated valley must have been the site of the refuge cities of Manco and his sons. How else could the presence of Spanish horseshoes be explained? The roofing tile we had found earlier strengthens this hypothesis. . . .

Monday, July 13, Espíritu Pampa. New Discoveries

At dawn we send Ascensión down river with a can of salt, a machete and a small axe from our stores (money has absolutely no value to these isolated tribes) to barter with the Machiguengas. He is instructed to speak with the chief (tribal custom forbids them from giving out their names for fear of losing their souls, so he is to address the chef as Mariano) and to try to obtain information about ruins. Ascensión is told to give the items to the chief if he agrees to tells us of the whereabouts of ancient remains. This will be our only chance to make contact, we are told. Once our man enters the "Machi" camp they will fade away in the jungle and not come out.

I set out with a dozen men to explore the pampas. Packs of wild pigs, forty or fifty head each, are said to frequent the jungle plains. Vicious when disturbed, they will charge a man. If he attempts to escape by climbing a tree, they uproot it and try to tear the man apart. I have the rifle and ammunition broken out. We head for the bridge we had seen two days before, where we start cutting trails into the dense vegetation. I fan the men out and shortly one of them reports he has come to a wall, below the fountain with three spouts. It turns out to be another stone fountain with a single waterspout; but better worked than the first. . . . Incredible! Not more than twenty feet from the other fountain and no one was aware of its existence, so thick was the tangle of jungle growth.

We find another stone wall directly behind the fountain. It proves to be a walled avenue of some kind. It is under a thorn forest so thick we would have been hours cutting through it. We give up trying

to breach it and turn our attention to the other side of the bridge where one of the men has found a retaining wall of an elevated group of Inca houses. Across from this group we fall into a depression and discover we have accidentally stumbled into a sunken group of Inca buildings under a mass of twisting vines and growth. It is below street level, completely walled. An hour of exploring the colossal group reveals inner streets, stairways and eighteen independent rooms. The group measures a stupendous 297 feet long! A canal with flowing water runs on one side. Tons of dead vegetation top the old ruins. One Inca house measuring 40 feet long by 18 feet wide is graced with thirteen niches and a broken doorway. The stones are cemented with adobe, as with the Spanish Palace. The architecture is Inca, but strangely different. Clearing the site, we discover some twenty odd circular buildings 15 to 20 feet in diameter. My men show surprise at finding these ruins.

We scramble back up to the upper wall over which we had come and find it is a walled passage 15 feet wide. We cut our way over this street for 300 feet until we reach the upper walls of the long structure observed the day before. Making our way blindly along the inner walls we come to a slab of white stone, which appears to have been some kind of altar. Outside we find an elevated platform some 150 feet long by 115 feet wide. Atop the walled structure sit two Inca buildings with three rooms, each topped by jungle. We find evidence that the wall of irregular stones had been covered with a red ceramic-like stucco or terra-cotta. Between this unusual find and the long buildings we had chanced on, we found a huge boulder weighing hundreds of tons. It is topped by a great *metapalo* tree whose bole is 12 feet in diameter and covered with layers of moss and tropical vegetation. The buttress roots of the great tree enclose the boulder in a tenacious grip like arms of an octopus. The forest is so dark and dense it takes a long time and much effort to uncover a stone platform which supports the large stone. A stone stairway and walled avenue lead to two rectangular Inca buildings below the big boulder. The building materials used in construction are rough, white limestone blocks, but the corners of the buildings are hand-hewn and well-cut. But so much of the construction is covered with vegetation and displaced by the numerous vines that have dislodged the stonework, it is difficult to determine exact dimensions (field sketches were made at a later date when the buildings were cleared and the huge tree covering the elevated boulder cut away. The latter was found to measure nearly 65 feet long and 20 feet wide and oriented north to south). . . .

A hundred feet later, we come to three terraces. The outer wall is nearly 300 feet long. Together they staircase up 25 feet high. The top is gained with difficulty. We approach a wall, clear some growth away with our curvos, then take a stairway that leads to a spacious courtyard, now a wild garden of exotic tropical flowers, lianas, fern and palm trees. Seven houses, their walls in ruins, rise up in the center of the terraced citadel in an atmosphere of deathly silence (in keeping with the mood of the machetemen).

We drop back down to the road and soon come to another group of rectangular buildings built atop a terraced platform 306 by 178 feet. The men chop away some of the growth that clings to the walls of large stones and then we jump back to the floor of the jungle and resume our search for other ruins.

The road we have been following comes to a halt. Rather than retrace our steps, we decide to keep going in the same direction hoping to pick it up again. I have the men spread out. It is a half hour before we find two small Inca houses perched on a promontory overlooking a river, and another group of buildings. The stonework is of better quality than what we have seen before. It is evident that the cut white limestone blocks had once fit snugly together, although many had now been broken by feeder vines that had wormed their way between the stones and pried them apart. One of the buildings, a rectangular construction with two doorways, guards a green-lit temple, a high elevated bulwark of stone consisting of rooms with niches and fallen door lintels, inner courtyards and enclosures. It must have been very impressive when the Incas lived here. A large huaca boulder rests beside one of the walls. It looks as if it may have fallen from the top of the platform wall. A magnificent *matapalo* tree with a spreading crown some one hundred feet above our heads locks one of the walls in a grip of gnarled roots. Some of the rocks are squeezed out of place by its vice-like grip. Rattan vines hang down from its upper branches, forming a screen through which we must cut our way....

We return down to the lower group of white stone ruins and I put the men to work clearing so plans and a photographic record can be made. Watching the first sunlight fall upon these ancient walls after a lapse of several centuries is a memorable experience. The white granite blocks, covered by thin layers of delicate lichen, take on a ghostly appearance. An ominous quiet falls over the jungle as the axemen bite into green wood. The forest seems to shudder. The men chop at the base of a tall tree until it hangs suspended from a spiderweb of vines, like a tottering mast of a ship. Machetes glint in the sun. Vines snap. The tree falls. Leaves flutter earthward, caught in shafts of light. Thin, diamond-marked snakes coil like corkscrews and slither for cover.

For the first time I realize what we have found. We are in the heart of an ancient Inca city. Is this Manco's Vilcabamba—the lost city of the Incas? I am certain we are in parts of it. I experience an overwhelming sense of the history the ruins represent. For four hundred years they have remained in the realm of legend. Some men doubted they existed. But I always knew they were there, somewhere, awaiting discovery. To me they were the most important historical remains in Peru. Important because Manco was a glorious hero who gave dignity to Peru when all was lost. Important because so many great names had looked for them. Some would expect to find cyclopean walls covered with sheets of gold, or finely cut stone of the classic Cuzco style. Old Vilcabamba wasn't this at all. She was old and worn. The walls of her buildings were toppled, covered with thick, decaying vegetable matter; their foundations under tons of slide and ooze. She had been put to the torch by the Incas who had built her and ransacked by the Spaniards who were looking for gold. Four centuries of wild jungle had twisted that part which remained. But she had not lost her dignity.

One could easily see she had been a great metropolis, a colossus of the jungle. A wave of melancholy swept over me. It would require an army to clear these ruins properly; cost a fortune to restore the buildings to their original form, and they were so far from civilization that it might never be accomplished. The city represented everything for which the Incas stood. It was a monument to their industry, their struggle with nature, their fight for freedom against overpowering odds. This was immortal Vilcabamba—that legendary city of a thousand history books. If I never succeeded in finding another city it would not matter. Legend had been turned into history.

GENE SAVOY
Antisuyo: The Search for the Lost Cities of the Amazon, 1970

IN THE CONDOR'S SHADOW

In introducing Chilean poet Pablo Neruda's Alturas de Macchu Picchu *to English-speaking readers, Robert Pring-Mill stated without equivocation: "Neruda is one of the greatest poets writing in Spanish today, and* The Heights of Macchu Picchu *is his finest poem." A product of Neruda's middle period—written two decades after* Twenty Poems, *the volume that established his reputation, and three decades before his career was capped by a Nobel Prize for Literature—*Macchu Picchu *echoes many of Neruda's major themes, among them the primitive beauty of the Andean landscape and the importance of primitive traditions. With the sixth section, the first of three reprinted below, the poet begins his ascent to the citadel—and, simultaneously, his journey backward through time to the moment of the city's creation.*

Then up the ladder of the earth I climbed
through the barbed jungle's thickets
until I reached you Macchu Picchu.

Tall city of stepped stone,
home at long last of whatever earth
had never hidden in her sleeping clothes.
In you two lineages that had run parallel
met where the cradle both of man and light
rocked in a wind of thorns.

Mother of stone and sperm of condors.

High reef of the human dawn.

Spade buried in primordial sand.

This was the habitation, this is the site:
here the fat grains of maize grew high
to fall again like red hail.

The fleece of the vicuña was carded here
to clothe men's loves in gold, their tombs and mothers,
the king, the prayers, the warriors.

Up here men's feet found rest at night

near eagles' talons in the high
meat-stuffed eyries. And in the dawn
with thunder steps they trod the thinning mists,
touching the earth and stones that they might recognize
that touch come night, come death.

I gaze at clothes and hands,
traces of water in the booming cistern,
a wall burnished by the touch of a face
that witnessed with my eyes the earth's carpet of tapers,
oiled with my hands the vanished wood:
for everything, apparel, skin, pots, words,
wine, loaves, has disappeared,
fallen to earth.

And the air came in with lemon blossom fingers
to touch those sleeping faces:
a thousand years of air, months, weeks of air,
blue wind and iron cordilleras—
these came with gentle footstep hurricanes
cleansing the lonely precinct of the stone.

Come up with me, American love.

Kiss these secret stones with me.
The torrential silver of the Urubamba
makes the pollen fly to its golden cup.
The hollow of the bindweed's maze,
the petrified plant, the inflexible garland,
soar above the silence of these mountain coffers.
Come, diminutive life, between the wings
of the earth, while you, cold, crystal in the hammered air,
thrusting embattled emeralds apart,
O savage waters, fall from the hems of snow.
Love, love, until the night collapses
from the singing Andes flint
down to the dawn's red knees,
come out and contemplate the snow's blind son.

O Wilkamayu of the sounding looms,
when you rend your skeins of thunder
in white foam clouds of wounded snow,
when your south wind falls like an avalanche
roaring and belting to arouse the sky,
what language do you wake in an ear
freed but a moment from your Andean spume?

Who caught the lightning of the cold,
abandoned it, chained to the heights,

dealt out among its frozen tears,
brandished upon its nimble swords—
its seasoned stamens pummeled hard—
led to a warrior's bed,
hounded to his rocky conclusions?
What do your harried scintillations whisper?
Did your sly, rebellious flash
go traveling once, populous with words?
Who wanders grinding frozen syllables,
black languages, gold-threaded banners,
fathomless mouths and trampled cries
in your tenuous arterial waters?

Who goes dead-heading blossom eyelids
come to observe us from the far earth?
Who scatters dead seed clusters
dropping from your cascading hands
to bed their own disintegration here
in coal's geology?

Who has flung down the branches of these chains
and buried once again our leave-takings?
Love, love, do not come near the border,
avoid adoring this sunken head:
let time exhaust all measure
in its abode of broken overtures—
here, between cliffs and rushing waters,
take to yourself the air among these passes,
the laminated image of the wind,
the blind canal threading high cordilleras,
dew with its bitter greetings,
and climb, flower by flower, through the thicknesses
trampling, the coiling lucifer.

In this steep zone of flint and forest,
green stardust, jungle-clarified,
Mantur, the valley, cracks like a living lake
or a new level of silence.

Come to my very being, to my own dawn,
into crowned solitudes.
The fallen kingdom survives us all this while.

And on this dial the condor's shadow
cruises as ravenous as would a pirate ship.

Stone within stone, and man, where was he?
Air within air, and man, where was he?
Time within time, and man, where was he?

Were you also the shattered fragment
of indecision, of hollow eagle
which, through the streets of today, in the old tracks,
through the leaves of accumulated autumns,
goes pounding at the soul into the tomb?
Poor hand, poor foot, and poor, dear life . . .
The days of unraveled light
in you, familiar rain
falling on feast-day banderillas,
did they grant, petal by petal, their dark nourishment
to such an empty mouth?
Famine, coral of mankind,
hunger, secret plan, root of the woodcutters,
famine, did your jagged reef dart up
to those high, side-slipping towers?

I question you, salt of the highways,
show me the trowel; allow me, architecture,
to fret stone stamens with a little stick,
climb all the steps of air into the emptiness,
scrape the intestine until I touch mankind.
Macchu Picchu, did you lift
stone above stone on a groundwork of rags?
coal upon coal and, at the bottom, tears?
fire-crested gold, and in that gold, the bloat
dispenser of this blood?

Let me have back the slave you buried here!
Wrench from these lands the stale bread
of the poor, prove me the tatters
on the serf, point out his window.
Tell me how he slept when alive,
whether he snored,
his mouth agape like a dark scar
worn by fatigue into the wall.
That wall, that wall! If each stone floor
weighed down his sleep, and if he fell
beneath them, as if beneath a moon, with all that sleep!

Ancient America, bride in her veil of sea,
your fingers also,
from the jungle's edges to the rare height of gods,
under the nuptial banners of light and reverence,
blending with thunder from the drums and lances,
your fingers, your fingers also—
that bore the rose in mind and hairline of the cold,
the blood-drenched breast of the new crops translated
into the radiant weave of matter and adamantine hollows—
with them, with them, buried America, were you in that great depth,
the bilious gut, hoarding the eagle hunger?

PABLO NERUDA
The Heights of Macchu Picchu, 1945

REFERENCE

Chronology of the Conquest

D. FRAN.ᶜᵒ PIZARRO CONQUIS.ᴰᴼᴿ D. PERᵁ.

In a sense there is only one date of consequence in the history of Machu Picchu—July 24, 1911, the day Hiram Bingham and his Indian guide, Melchor Arteaga, first laid eyes on the "Lost City of the Incas." All antecedent dates are a matter of conjecture; all subsequent dates are of little import except to professional archaeologists. What follows is a more useful sort of chronology—of the brief, bloody interval known as the Conquest, during which a small band of avaricious adventurers succeeded in subduing the greatest culture South America ever produced.

c. 1410	Peruvian mountain tribe led by ruler known as the Inca extends suzerainty to include two headwaters of the Amazon, the Apurimac and the Urubamba
1438	Pachacuti Inca conquers the Chanca tribe near Cuzco, ushering in the Inca empire's golden age
c. 1450	Subjugation of Lupaca and Colla tribes; empire extended south as far as Lake Titicaca
c. 1470	Birth of Francisco Pizarro
1493	Tawantin-suyu, the Inca "Land of the Four Quarters," at its imperial apogee; from capital at Cuzco the Inca rules a domain that stretches from Quito (in modern Ecuador) to the southern tip of Chile—a distance of 2,500 miles
1513	Vasco Núñez de Balboa discovers the Pacific Ocean
1519	Conquest of Mexico's Aztec empire by Hernán Cortés; founding of city of Panama on Pacific coast of isthmus
1524	Francisco Pizarro's first Pacific expedition reaches San Juan River
1527	Pizarro's second expedition sights coastline of "Birú"—Peru—before establishing an encampment on Isla del Gallo, off the northern coast; foray to Gulf of Guayaquil and Túmbes suggests empire of enormous wealth
1528	Word reaches royal palace at Tumibamba of strange ships sighted off coast of Peru
1529	Returning to his native Spain, Pizarro obtains a *capitulación* from the queen to conquer Peru to a distance of 200 leagues south of the Gulf of Guayaquil; sets out from Panama the following year

1532	Pizarro and his two brothers, Hernando and Gonzalo, reach tip of northern Peru with a complement of 168 men, 62 horses, and 2 pieces of artillery; Spaniards capture Atahualpa Inca at Cajamarca; while a prisoner of the Spanish, has his rival, Huascar, murdered	Apr. 1538	Hernando Pizarro defeats Almagro at Las Salinas, transports him back to Cuzco, and has him executed (July)
Jan. 1533	Hernando Pizarro leads a party of conquistadores to Pachacamac, where they sack a pre-Inca temple and loot its gold statuary	Feb. 1539	Surrender of Tiso Yupanqui and collapse of rebellion
		Apr. 1539	Vilcabamba invaded by Gonzalo Pizarro
Feb. 1533	Three-man reconnaisance party sets out for Cuzco	Oct. 1539	Surrender of Villac Umu, executed one month later at Yucay along with Cura Ocllo, Tiso, other commanders
Mar. 1533	On Atahualpa's orders, Indians begin assembling his ransom—tons of gold and silver—from all corners of the empire	July 1541	Francisco Pizarro assassinated by Almagrists in Lima
July 1533	Distribution of Atahualpa's ransom to conquistadores, who execute their royal prisoner 10 days later	1542	Manco Inca provides sanctuary for Almagrist fugitives at Vitcos following their defeat; in Barcelona, King Charles of Spain issues New Laws governing his empire's New World holdings
Aug. 1533	Coronation of Atahualpa's successor, Tupac Huallpa Inca, at Cajamarca; puppet ruler joins invaders on their southward march, his presence their protection	1544	Manco murdered by Spanish renegades at Vitcos; Gonzalo Pizarro enters Lima, driving out forces of Núñez Vela, first viceroy of Peru
Oct. 1533	Sudden death of Tupac Huallpa, possibly due to poison administered by followers of Huascar, at Jauja	1545	Discovery of silver lode at Potosí
		1546	Gonzalo Pizarro defeats and kills Núñez Vela
Nov. 1533	Pizarro and Diego de Almagro enter Cuzco in triumph	1547	Alvarado's forces beaten at Huarina by Gonzalo Pizarro
Dec. 1533	Coronation of Manco Inca, Atahualpa's half-brother, in Cuzco	1548	At Jaquijahuana, Pedro de la Gasca defeats Gonzalo Pizarro; negotiations follow between Gasca and regents of Sayri-Tupac at Vilcabamba
Feb. 1534	Inca attack, led by Quisquis, repelled by Spanish forces garrisoned at Jauja; Pedro de Alvarado lands in Ecuador	1549	Death of Paullu Inca
		1557	After protracted negotiations, Sayri-Tupac is persuaded to leave Vilcabamba and meet the Spanish viceroy in Lima
Mar. 1534	Francisco Pizarro "founds" Spanish municipality at Cuzco	1560	Death of Sayri-Tupac; Titu Cusi crowned in Vilcabamba
July 1535	Almagro's expedition departs with the Inca prince Paullu for Chile	1566	Treaty of Acobamba between Titu Cusi and Spaniards signed at Vilcabamba
Oct. 1535	Manco Inca, attempting to flee Cuzco, is captured and imprisoned	1567	Titu Cusi performs act of submission to Spain; his son, Quispe Titu, baptized at Vilcabamba
May 1536	Manco's troops attack Cuzco, setting fire to city; Juan Pizarro dies as Spanish recapture fortress of Sacsayhuaman	1571	Titu Cusi dies of an apparent stroke and is succeeded by Tupac Amaru
Apr. 1537	Almagro relieves siege of Cuzco and replaces Hernando Pizarro as commandant	1572	Viceroy Toledo proclaims war of "fire and blood" to eradicate Inca and followers at Vilcabamba; Spanish expeditionary force reaches jungle stronghold in June and discovers it has been put to torch; Tupac Amaru captured, returned in chains to Cuzco, and executed
July 1537	Rodrigo Orgóñez pursues Manco to Vitcos, which Inca abandons in favor of a new city, Vilcabamba; Paullu crowned puppet in Cuzco		

Guide to Machu Picchu

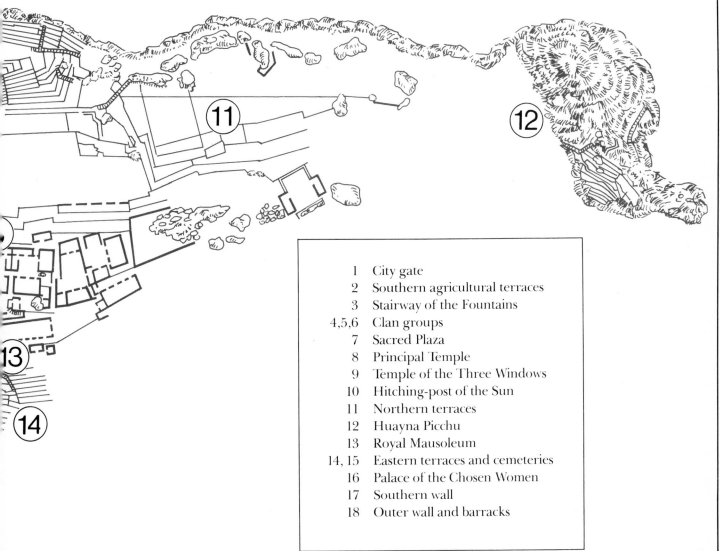

1	City gate
2	Southern agricultural terraces
3	Stairway of the Fountains
4,5,6	Clan groups
7	Sacred Plaza
8	Principal Temple
9	Temple of the Three Windows
10	Hitching-post of the Sun
11	Northern terraces
12	Huayna Picchu
13	Royal Mausoleum
14, 15	Eastern terraces and cemeteries
16	Palace of the Chosen Women
17	Southern wall
18	Outer wall and barracks

Wilhelmina Reyinga

*Machu Picchu's main gate—
an artist's conjecture
based on Bingham's notes.*

Machu Picchu is not most of the things its discoverer, Hiram Bingham, claimed it was. It is not the mythic pre-Inca city of Tampu-tocco, the presumptive primordial home of the founders of the Peruvian empire. It is not the burial place of Pachacuti, the mighty warlord whose campaigns of conquest established the Inca empire. It is not a sacred necropolis, housing the mortal remains of countless *mamaconas,* the "chosen women" who served the royal household. And, above all, it is not the last refuge of Manco Inca or the nexus of that hapless ruler's post-Conquest government-in-exile.

Indeed, Machu Picchu is less important, historically speaking, than many far less famous Inca ruins. Bingham, who visited many of those ruins and discovered a number of the most important—among them what would later prove to be the true last citadel of the Incas—devoted the last four decades of his life to inflating his claims for Machu Picchu. And even as he exaggerated the significance of what he had found, others were unearthing evidence to refute his assertions. The controversy that surrounds Bingham's claims on behalf of Machu Picchu cannot diminish the splendor of the site itself, however. It is, quite simply, magnificent.

Machu Picchu was a remarkable natural fortress when the Incas occupied it five centuries ago, and the very topographical features that made it unique then have conspired to preserve its singularity to this day. It is a good deal easier to reach Machu Picchu today than it was in 1911, the year of Bingham's expedition, but even so the region's forbidding terrain has enabled South

America's most famous archaeological site to resist the depredations common to tourist attractions. As a result, modern visitors who reach the heights that Bingham and his Indian guide first ascended on the morning of July 24, 1911, have little trouble imagining how Machu Picchu must have looked to the Yale-educated explorer. Or how it must have looked to its builders.

Whatever its history, and whatever purpose it may have served, Machu Picchu is indisputably the most spectacular of Inca sites, perched as it is some 2,000 feet above the roaring waters of the Urubamba River on a knife-sharp ridge of exposed rock, a single vertebra in the spine of the Vilcabamba cordillera. To reach this Inca aerie one must leave Cuzco, 46 miles to the southeast, by train in the chill predawn. Throughout the morning the narrow-gauge train descends the long Anta valley, passing the spot where, in 1531, Atahualpa's generals defeated his rival Huascar and seized control of the empire he would soon lose to the conquistadores, even then approaching the western shores of his realm. In this same valley the little train chugs past the place where, in 1548, the renegade Gonzalo Pizarro suffered defeat at the hands of royalists.

As the train begins its descent into the densely forested valley of the Urubamba, following that river westward, it passes the ruins of Ollantaytambo, the greatest of the Incas' frontier temples. The final stage of the journey, the ascent to the site itself, is accomplished by passenger bus on a government-built roadway, El Camino de Hiram Bingham, that winds upward from the railhead to a tourist hotel at the summit.

The first-time visitor cannot help but notice how truly spectacular Machu Picchu's natural defenses are—and how isolating. It is as difficult to imagine encroaching civilization's finding a way of scaling the steep flanks of this arete as it is to envision an invading army's finding a way up. The ruins can be approached with ease only from the south, there being but one formal entrance to the city (**1**, on the diagram on pp. 164–65). And it was, during Inca times, triply guarded—by a double row of stepped retaining walls, by a dry moat, and, finally, by a heavy wooden gate (see sketch above). To the north, east, and west, nature has provided defenses less easily breached than any humans could have devised: the Urubamba, doubling back on itself, isolates the ridge on which Machu Picchu stands from the surrounding mountaintops. To reach the city invaders would have to descend to the valley floor and then scale the sheer cliff-faces, which are clad in all but impenetrable foliage.

Within the city itself are numerous structures ranging from one-room private dwellings to far larger public buildings. Some are constructed of granite ashlars, cut with the craft and fitted with the finesse that distinguishes the peerless work of Inca masons. The thatched roofs and wooden roofbeams of these structures have long since rotted away and today only their fittings remain, but from these we can easily envision how the original buildings must have looked (see sketch at top right). What the tourist may fail to appreciate at first is that many of the buildings of Machu Picchu, hut and temple alike, served a dual purpose, the secondary one being that of

166

A typical dwelling at Machu Picchu as it may have looked in Inca times.

defense: their windowless outer walls providing a barrier against invasion.

How long Machu Picchu could have withstood attack is open to question. Its water supply was probably not adequately protected against a concerted attack, and its food stores were probably insufficient to feed the populace during a protracted siege. But the question is almost certainly an academic one, for then as now Machu Picchu must be approached on foot and single file, and it is hard to conceive of even the most determined and enterprising commander's managing to assemble an invasion force in such a place.

To the right, as one surveys the city from its principal gate, stretch the irrigated agricultural terraces, or *andenes* (**2**), that once supplied the inhabitants of Machu Picchu with maize, beans, yams, and other foodstuffs. Directly below, across an open upper plaza strewn with massive boulders, is the so-called Stairway of the Fountains (**3**), the head of the citadel's ingenious aqueduct, which brings fresh water to Machu Picchu from almost a mile away. The stairway drops, in sixteen huge "steps," through the lower city, carrying potable water to every clan group, or residential ward (**4, 5, 6**), in the complex.

At the upper city's northwest corner lies the Sacred Plaza (**7**), location of Machu Picchu's most hallowed structures. To the north stands what Hiram Bingham called the Principal Temple (**8**), whose distinguishing features are its floor, paved with coarse white sand, and what is presumed to be an altar made of a single mighty ashlar measuring 14 feet in length and 5 in height. At the Sacred Plaza's eastern edge is

the best-known building in all of Machu Picchu, the Temple of the Three Windows (**9**). In actual fact its three walls contain five apertures—the fourth exposure is open to the plaza—but three of these are of a size and shape rarely encountered in Inca architecture and those openings give the temple its name.

In this same quadrant but further west we find the gnomon known as *inti-huatana*, the Hitching-post of the Sun (**10**), which can be reached from the Sacred Plaza via a connecting gallery and a flight of stone steps. This stepped platform, carved from a single slab of granite, figured prominently in Inca religion, which recognized a wide panoply of nature gods but held Inti, the sun god, supreme among them. In attempting to convey a sense of how sacrosanct this site was to the Incas, Bingham himself was to note:

A primitive folk so extremely dependent on the kindly behavior of the sun as were the Peruvian highlanders must have been in terror each year, as the shadows lengthened and the sun went farther and farther north, that he would never return but would leave them to perish of cold and hunger. Hence it seems likely that these short stone posts [*inti-huatanas*] represented the post to which a mystical rope was tied by the priests to prevent the sun going too far away and getting lost.

Other terraces (**11**) are found along the city's northern perimeter. Beyond them, at the north terminus of the granite saddle upon which Machu Picchu sits, rises Huayna Picchu (**12**), a sugarloaf surmounted by a watchtower

from which Inca lookouts could see far down the Urubamba valley.

The return circuit from Huayna Picchu to Machu Picchu's main gate takes the visitor through the upper city and past the structure known as the Royal Mausoleum (**13**), held to be the place where the fabric-swaddled, gold-bedecked, mummified remains of the Incas' deceased monarchs were preserved. We know that the desiccated bodies of Inca rulers were housed in splendid palaces in Cuzco, the capital of the Inca empire, and displayed daily in the central square. Whether such a rite was actually observed at Machu Picchu is a matter of conjecture. In any event, such elaborate funerary practices applied only to royalty; commoners were buried in the cemeteries that dot the city's broad eastern terraces (**14, 15**).

By mounting the Stairway of the Fountains, one reaches the semicircular structure that Bingham dubbed the Temple of the Sun. He speculated that the preponderance of female skeletons found at Machu Picchu suggest that this was the home of the *mamaconas*, or chosen women, whose lifetime obligation it was to serve the personal needs of the Inca himself. Whether or not the building in question ever served such a function, it does provide an admirable vantage from which to survey the great terraces that fall away on the far side of the citadel's southern wall (**17**). Across them can be seen the remains of Machu Picchu's outermost walls (**18**), and beyond this last perimeter can be seen the sublime panorama of the Vilcabamba cordillera, whose arresting beauty threatens at every turn to beggar the splendor of Machu Picchu itself.

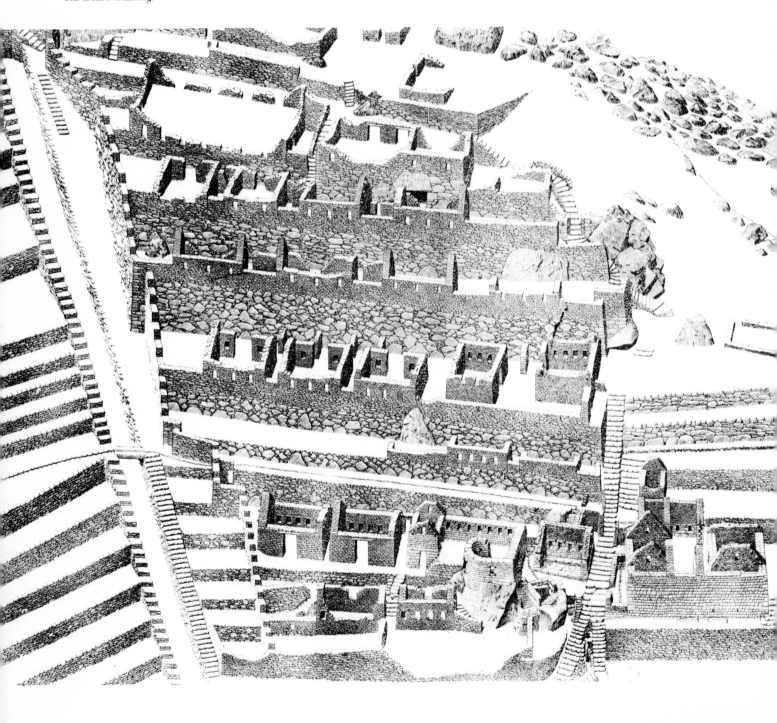

*Bird's-eye view of Machu
Picchu showing the so-called
King's Group, to the right
of the Principal Staircase,
with the Semicircular Temple,
or Torreón, to the left in
this artist's rendering.*

Selected Bibliography

Bennett, Wendell C. "Machu Picchu, the most famous Inca ruin." *Natural History,* 35, pt. 1. New York: American Museum of Natural History, 1935.

Bingham, Hiram. "The Story of Machu Picchu." *National Geographic Magazine,* February 1915.

———. *In the Wonderland of Peru.* Washington, D.C.: Judd and Detweiler, 1913.

———. *Lost City of the Incas.* New York: Duell, Sloan and Pearce, 1948.

———. *Machu Picchu, A Citadel of the Incas.* New Haven: Yale University Press, 1930.

Fejos, Paul. *Archeological Explorations in the Cordillera Vilcabamba, Southeastern Peru.* New York: Viking Fund Publications in Anthropology (No. 3), 1944.

Hemming, John. *The Conquest of the Incas.* New York: Harcourt Brace Jovanovich, 1970.

Kubler, George. "Machu Picchu." *Perspecta,* 6, pp. 48-55. New Haven: Yale University Press, 1960.

Mason, J. Alden. *The Ancient Civilizations of Peru.* London: Harmondsworth, 1957.

Neruda, Pablo. *The Heights of Macchu Picchu.* London: Jonathan Cape, 1966.

Savoy, Gene. *Antisuyo—The Search for the Lost Cities of the Amazon.* New York: Simon and Schuster, 1970.

von Hagen, Victor W. *A Guide to Machu Picchu.* New York: Frederick Farnam Associates, 1949.

Acknowledgments and Picture Credits

The Editors would like to express their particular appreciation to Michael Lubell for making available the remarkable photographs of the late George Holton. In addition, the Editors would like to thank the following people:
Hiram III and Alfred Bingham; Charlie Holland; Henry La Farge; Barbara Shattuck at the National Geographic Society; and George Vicas.

The title or description of each picture appears after the page number (boldface), followed by its location. Photographic credits appear in parentheses. The following abbreviations are used:

AMNH—American Museum of National History
  (HB)—Courtesy of the Family of Hiram Bingham and the National Geographic Society
  (GH)—George Holton
  MAI—Museum of the American Indian
  NYPL—New York Public Library

ENDPAPERS Embroidered mantle, Ica culture, Peru. AMNH HALF TITLE Symbol designed by Jay J. Smith Studio FRONTISPIECE (GH) **9** Wooden *kero,* Inca, Cuzco, Peru. (MAI) **10-11** Indian women, c. 1912 (HB) **12-13** Half-feather poncho, Chimu culture, Peru. Textile Museum, Washington, D. C.

CHAPTER I **15** (HB) **16** Urubamba River (R. Lans Christensen) **18–19** top Hiram Bingham at Machu Picchu (HB) **19** bottom Bingham at Pampaconas, August, 1911. (HB) **20–21** West side of Machu Picchu. Top: July 21, 1912. Bottom: August 17, 1912. Both: (HB) **22–23** Inca roadway at Sacsayhuaman (Hans Silvester—Rapho-Photo Researchers) **24–25** (Left: (HB) Right: (GH) **26–27** All: Poma de Ayala, *Nueva Corónica . . . ,* c. 1610. Kongelige Biblioteck, Copenhagen. **28–29** (GH) **30** Main city gate. (HB) **30–31** Entrance to clan groups. (HB) **32–33** (GH)

CHAPTER II **35** (HB) **36** Stone head, Cuzco, Peru. Museo de America, Madrid (Oroñoz) **37** Lake Titicaca (GH) **38** Map by Wilhelmina Reyinga **41** Machu Picchu from Huayna Picchu (Hans Silvester—Rapho-Photo Researchers) **42-43** Both: Poma de Ayala, *Nueva Corónica . . . ,* c. 1610. Kongelige Bibliotek, Copenhagen. **44** House of the Princess and Torreón (GH) **45** Royal Mausoleum (GH) **46-47** Temple of the Three Windows (HB) **49** Gold female figurine, Inca, Peru. MAI **52-53** Hitching-post of the Sun (GH)

CHAPTER III **55** (HB) **56 & 57** Both: Cuzco. Both: (R. Lans Christensen) **58** Temple of the Sun, Cuzco. Laurent Saint-Cricq, *Voyage à Travers l'Amerique du Sud,* Paris, 1869. Rare Book Division, NYPL **59** Jesuit monastery, Cuzco. (HB) **60-61** Calle Hatunrumiyoc, Cuzco. (GH) **62-63** Both: Poma de Ayala, *Nueva Corónica . . . ,* c. 1610. Kongelige Bibliotek, Copenhagen. **64-65** All: (GH) **68-69** Sacsayhuaman (GH)

CHAPTER IV **71** (HB) **72** Embossed gold crown, Chavín culture, Peru. MAI **73** Rendering of Raimondi Stele. **75** top Crouching tiger vessel; center, Portrait jar; bottom, Spouted vessel with mountain scene. All: Mochica culture, Peru. All: MAI **76-77** left All: Pottery figures, Mochica, Peru. All: Metropolitan Museum of Art, Gift of Nathan Cummings, 1964. **77** right Male captive, Mochica. MAI **78** top Two-spouted jar, Nazca culture, Peru; bottom left, Two-spouted jar with wild cat decoration, Nazca; bottom right, Gold-sheet mummy mask, Nazca. All: MAI **79** Woven pouch, Nazca. MAI **80** Maria Reiche blueprinting rock drawings. (Dr. Georg Gerster—Photo Researchers) **81** Reiche cleaning Nazca bird figure. (Dr. Georg Gerster—Photo Researchers) **83** Tiahuanaco figure (HB) **84** Gold mummy mask, Chimu culture, Peru. MAI **85** Gold and silver ceremonial cup, Chimu. MAI **86** Silver effigy vessel, Chimu. Metropolitan Museum of Art, Michael Rockefeller Collection of Primitive Art. **88-89** Painted gold funerary mask, Chimu. Metropolitan Museum of Art, Gift of Mrs. Harold L. Bache, 1974.

CHAPTER V   **91** (HB) **92** Stone and shell-inlaid gold ear plugs, Mochica. Metropolitan Museum of Art, Gift of Mrs. Harold L. Bache, 1966. **92** Bridge spanning Apurímac River. (Hans Silvester—Rapho-Photo Researchers) **94** Whistling seed pod pot, Mochica. MAI **95** Corn pot, Mochica. MAI **96** top Indian girl, Cuzco; bottom; Vendor in market place in La Paz, Bolivia. Both: (GH) **97** Mother and child, Chincheros, Peru. (GH) **99-100** Detail of shirt, coastal Inca, 15th century. Metropolitan Museum of Art, Michael Rockefeller Collection of Primitive Art. **101** Polychrome *kero* in shape of puma head, Inca. MAI

CHAPTER VI   **103** (HB) **104** Silver basin- memorial to Francisco Pizarro, Peru, 18th century. The Brooklyn Museum, Carll de Silver Fund. **105** Watercolor of Atahualpa Inca from Spanish album of Inca rulers. Gilcrease Institute. **106** Antonio de Herrera, *Decades* . . . , Antwerp, 1728. **109** Both: Theodor de Bry, *America*, 1590. Rare Book Division, NYPL. **113** D.B.M. Compañon, *Trujillo del Peru* . . . , 1782-88. Biblioteca de Palacio Real, Madrid.

CHAPTER VII   **115** (HB) **117** Pizarro's battle standard. Museo del Ejercito, Madrid (Oroñoz) **119** Theodor de Bry, *America*, 1590. Rare Book Division, NYPL. **120** Zarate, *The Strange and Delectable History* . . . , London, 1581. Rare Book Division, NYPL. **122** Silver alpaca, Inca, c. 1450. MAI **123** (GH)

CHAPTER VIII   **125** (HB) **127** Watercolor of Manco Inca from Spanish album of Inca rulers. Gilcrease Institute. **129** Theodor de Bry, *America*, 1590. Rare Book Division, NYPL. **130** Poma de Ayala, *Nueva Corónica* . . . , c. 1610. Kongelige Bibliotek, Copenhagen. **133** Wooden *kero* of Spanish soldiers, Peru. Museo de America, Madrid (Oroñoz) **134-35** Both: Poma de Ayala, *Nueva Corónica* . . . , c. 1610. Kongelige Bibliotek, Copenhagen. **136** (GH)

MACHU PICCHU IN LITERATURE   All: Laurent Saint-Cricq, *Voyage à Travers l'Amerique du Sud*, Paris, 1869. NYPL

REFERENCE   **164-65** Diagram of Machu Picchu by Wilhelmina Reyinga. **166-67** Both: (HB) **168-69** (HB)

Index